THE

AIRCRAFT
MARKINGS

By JOHN W. R. TAYLOR

LONDON

Ian Allan Ltd

John W. R. Taylor who was responsible for *Civil Aircraft Markings* from the early days until 1978 sadly died on 12 December 1999 aged 77. From the very beginning the March publishing date for the pocket-sized annual was eagerly awaited by enthusiasts at the start of another season. John Taylor ensured that they were not disappointed and the popular book always maintained the same standard through the years. His efforts helped to generate an interest in civil aviation at a time when they were few facilities and even fewer books on the subject. John Taylor will be much missed by his friends and associates but he will not be forgotten.

de Havilland **COMET**

First published 1950
Reprinted 2000

ISBN 0 7110 2759 5

© Ian Allan Publishing Ltd 1950 / 2000

Published by Ian Allan Publishing

an imprint of Ian Allan Publishing Ltd, Terminal House, Station Approach, Shepperton, Surrey TW17 8AS.

Printed by Ian Allan Printing Ltd, Riverdene Business Park, Hersham, Surrey KT12 4RG.

Code: 0005/A

Introduction

MOST of us were aircraft " spotters " to some degree or other during the last war, from the Royal Observer Corps expert who could report a speck in the sky as a "Spitfire at 10,000ft. flying S.W." to the housewife who happily identified it by instinct as " one of ours."

The life and death urgency of wartime plane spotting has passed, but it kindled the spark of a fascinating hobby which is helping to fill public enclosures at our airports every fine Summer day with thousands of people, who want to know not merely that a Stratocruiser has four engines, but that the particular Stratocruiser in front of them belongs to B.O.A.C. and has just come over from America with 70 passengers, including film star Aurora Borealis, the " Alaskan Bombshell."

We do not claim that this book will tell you all that, but it *will* tell you the type of aircraft that you are looking at, who owns it and quite a lot about it. Furthermore, it is not intended just for the lucky few who can get to London Airport or Northolt, as it will be equally helpful to the many who look up as an aeroplane passes over their homes and think " What is it ?" Many who use it will devise their own methods of recording in it which registrations they have seen.

Every aircraft carries registration markings on its wings and fuselage, which distinguish it readily from all others, and this A.B.C. lists the markings of virtually every civil aircraft normally seen in British skies, including all foreign air liners which serve this country regularly. In this it is more comprehensive than its popular predecessor—the *A.B.C. of British Aircraft Markings*—as well as being, of course, bang up-to-date. It has also profited from criticism, both kind and otherwise, of the earlier book ; in particular, the British civil markings are arranged alphabetically instead of under the aircraft type names.

Anthony Fokker, the great Dutch aircraft designer, once said that " Flying will be here to stay only when it ceases to be an adventure." For thousands of people today, flying is just another means of getting from A to B quickly and comfortably. But there must always be adventure in a form of transport that can bring men and women from the furthermost ends of the earth in a matter of hours, over deserts, mountains, oceans and jungles rich in history and romance. If this little book helps just a few people to share more fully in this great adventure of flying it will have been very worth-while.

J.W.R.T.

AIRCRAFT NATIONALITY MARKINGS

AP	Pakistan	**OE**	Austria	**TC**	Turkey
CC	Chile	**OH**	Finland	**TF**	Iceland
CF	Canada	**OK**	Czecho-Slovakia	**URSS**	Russia
CS	Portugal	**OO**	Belgium	**VH**	Australia
EC	Spain	**OY**	Denmark	**VP**	E. & W. Africa
EI	Eire	**PH**	Netherlands	**VP-C**	Ceylon
EP	Iran	**PI**	Philippines	**VQ-C**	Cyprus
ET	Ethiopia	**PJ**	Neth. W. Indies	**VR-G**	Gibraltar
F	France	**PK**	Neth. E. Indies	**VR-H**	Hong Kong
G	Great Britain	**PP**	Brazil	**VT**	India
HA	Hungary	**PT**	Brazil	**XT**	China
HB	Switzerland	**RX**	Panama	**XY**	Burma
HS	Siam	**SA**	Saudi Arabia	**YI**	Iraq
I	Italy	**SE**	Sweden	**YR**	Roumania
LN	Norway	**SN**	Sudan	**YU**	Yugo-Slavia
LV	Argentina	**SP**	Poland	**YV**	Venezuela
LX	Luxembourg	**SR**	Syria	**ZK**	New Zealand
LZ	Bulgaria	**SU**	Egypt	**ZS**	South Africa
NC	U.S.A.	**SX**	Greece	**4X**	Israel

ABBREVIATIONS
used in this book

A.O.A.	American Overseas Airlines
Assoc.	Association
B.E.A.C.	British European Airways Corporation
B.O.A.C.	British Overseas Airways Corporation
C. I.	Channel Islands
Corp.	Corporation
D.H.	de Havilland
F.A.M.A.	Flota Aerea Mercante Argentina (Argentine Air Lines)
I.o.M.	Isle of Man
K.L.M.	Royal Dutch Airlines
M.C.A.	Ministry of Civil Aviation
M.o.S.	Ministry of Supply
P.A.A.	Pan American World Airways
U.L.A.A.	Ultra Light Aircraft Association
U.L.A.C.	Ultra Light Aero Club

British Civil Aircraft Registrations

(Correct to mid-June, 1950)

in alphabetical order

Registration	Type	Owner or Operator
G–EBKY	Sopwith Pup	Shuttleworth Trust
G–EBMB	Hawker Cygnet	Hawker Aircraft Co.
G–EBRN	Widgeon 3	N. C. Anderson
G–EBWD	D.H.60X Moth	Shuttleworth Trust
G–AAHW	Klemm L–25–1A	G. R. Lush
G–AAPZ	Desoutter	Shuttleworth Trust
G–AAWO	D.H.60 Moth	T. H. Marshall
G–AAYX	Southern Martlet	U.L.A.A.
G–AAZP	Puss Moth	Autowork (Winchester)
G–ABAG	D.H.60 Moth	P.M.A. Hull
G–ABDF	Puss Moth	J. M. Banks
G–ABEE	Avian 4M	H. R. A. Edwards
G–ABJJ	D.H. 60 Moth	Universal Flying Services
G–ABMB	Hawker Cygnet	Hawker Aircraft
G–ABMR	Hart 2	Hawker Aircraft
G–ABUS	Comper Swift	A. L. Cole
G–ABUU	Comper Swift	P/O Baneudale
G–ABWP	Arrow	Shuttleworth Trust
G–ABYA	D.H.60 Moth	M. C. Harley
G–ACCB	Fox Moth	Giro Aviation Co.
G–ACDI	Tiger Moth	Air Service Training
G–ACEJ	Fox Moth	Giro Aviation Co.
G–ACHP	Club Cadet	Saunders-Roe
G–ACIT	Dragon	Airways Aero Assoc.
G–ACKE	Avian 4m	H. M. Woodhams
G–ACLD	Blackburn B–2	Blackburn Aircraft
G–ACLL	Leopard Moth	C. P. L. Godsal
G–ACMA	Leopard Moth	de Havilland Aircraft Co.
G–ACMN	Leopard Moth	de Havilland Aircraft Co.
G–ACPP	Dragon Rapide	Yellow Air Taxis
G–ACRW	Leopard Moth	F. T. Bingham
G–ACTF	Swift	R. E. Clear
G–ACTJ	Leopard Moth	A. R. Frogley
G–ACUU	Cierva C.30A	Cierva Autogiro Co.
G–ACYE	Cierva C.30A	M. Maxwell-Channell
G–ACYO	Hawk Major	B. C. Barton & Son
G–ACYR	Dragon Rapide	Reid & Sigrist
G–ACZP	D.H.86B	Bowmaker
G–ADAB	Hawk Major	C. N. Cooper
G–ADAH	Dragon Rapide	E. L. Gander-Dower
G–ADBE	Pitcairn PA–19	
G–ADCV	Hawk Major	B. S. St. A. H. Hurle-Hobbs
G–ADDI	Dragon	Air Charter
G–ADFD	Cadet	
G–ADFH	Falcon	D. E. Bianchi

Registration	Type	Owner or Operator
G-ADGP	Hawk Speed Six	R. R. Paine
G-ADHE	Moth Major	S. H. Wood
G-ADIA	Tiger Moth	Brooklands Aviation
G-ADIH	Tiger Moth	L. D. Trappitt
G-ADIJ	Tiger Moth	Brooklands Aviation
G-ADJV	Hornet Moth	J. J. Lister
G-ADKC	Hornet Moth	J. H. Minet & Co.
G-ADKK	Hornet Moth	C. B. Mills
G-ADKM	Hornet Moth	Mrs. M. K. Wilberforce
G-ADLI	Falcon	L. T. E. Bradley
G-ADLY	Hornet Moth	Viscountess Mairi Bury
G-ADMJ	Hornet Moth	L. H. Ridell
G-ADMT	Hornet Moth	London Aero Club
G-ADMW	Hawk Major	T. Shipside
G-ADNB	Hornet Moth	West London Aero Services
G-ADND	Hornet Moth	W. D. Macpherson
G-ADNE	Hornet Moth	West London Aero Services
G-ADNL	Sparrowhawk	C. G. M. Alington
G-ADOK	Tiger Moth	Inter-City Air Services
G-ADOT	Hornet Moth	Herts & Essex Aero Club
G-ADPR	Gull	Percival Aircraft
G-ADPS	Swallow 2	Walker & Thompson
G-ADSK	Hornet Moth	E. D. Wynn
G-ADTD	Falcon	R. S. Turner
G-ADUF	D.H.86B	J. A. W. Hill
G-ADUH	D.H.86B	Bond Air Services
G-ADUR	Hornet Moth	London Aeroplane Club
G-ADVJ	D.H.86B	Bond Air Services
G-ADWT	Hawk Major	T. Shipside Ltd.
G-ADYS	Aeronca C.3	
G-ADZL	Falcon	Fairey Aviation Co.
G-AEAI	Cessna C.34	R. E. Dewhurst
G-AEAL	Dragon Rapide	Hunting Aerosurveys
G-AEBJ	Blackburn B.2	Blackburn Aircraft
G-AECC	Falcon Six	J. Rush
G-AECN	Burgoyne Stirling Dicer	
G-AEET	Hornet Moth	London Aero Club
G-AEGI	Heck 2C	J. Crammond
G-AEGN	Swallow 2	T. C. Sparrow
G-AEGO	Eagle 2	Wing Cdr. F. S. Cotton
G-AEKY	Hornet Moth	West London Aero Services
G-AELG	Swallow 2	Swansea & District Flying Club
G-AELO	Hornet Moth	Airborne Taxi Services
G-AELX	Aeronca C.3	R. R. Ward
G-AEMH	Dragon Rapide	G. Clifton
G-AEML	Dragon Rapide	Sir W. G. Armstrong Whitworth Aircraft
G-AEMW	Swallow 2	L. F. P. Walters
G-AENU	Wicko I	S./Ldr. J. T. Shaw.
G-AEOA	Puss Moth	Airways Aero Assoc.
G-AERN	Dragon Rapide	Gibralter Airways
G-AERV	Whitney Straight	H. W. H. Moore
G-AESE	Hornet Moth	Goodhew Aviation
G-AESP	Aeronca 100	Airways Aero Assoc.
G-AESR	Dragon Rapide	Airwork
G-AESV	Phoenix	A. R. Pilgrim
G-AESZ	Chilton D.W.I	L. W. Taylor

Registration	Type	Owner or Operator
G-AEUT	Praga	Flt. Lt. F. Bosworth
G-AEUZ	Whitney Straight	H. Tempest
G-AEVA	Whitney Straight	J. C. Rice
G-AEVG	Whitney Straight	Air Service Training
G-AEVL	Whitney Straight	Lady M. F. A. Vane-Tempest Stewart.
G-AEVS	Aeronca 100	Airways Aero Assoc.
G-AEVT	Aeronca 100	P. Simpson
G-AEWA	Whitney Straight	S. J. Burt
G-AEWI	Swallow 2	D. A. Doughty
G-AEWL	Dragon Rapide	Air Kruise (Kent)
G-AEWU	Aeronca 100	T. S. Gooch
G-AEWV	Aeronca 100	F. Gill
G-AEWY	Hornet Moth	G. & A. Morgan Trust
G-AEWZ	Dragonfly	V. H. Bellamy
G-AEXD	Aeronca 100	Airways Aero Assoc.
G-AEXY	Taylor Cub	F. R. Evans
G-AEYC	Vega Gull	Lambskin Exports
G-AEYE	Percival Q.6	C. G. M. Alington
G-AEZF	Scion Junior	S. S. Caro
G-AEZG	Hornet Moth	Flightways
G-AEZM	Swallow 2	D. Kirk
G-AFAY	Falcon	Hawker Aircraft
G-AFBC	Vega Gull	Lady Sherborne
G-AFBF	Falcon	Cunliffe-Owen Aircraft
G-AFBY	Cessna C.34	W. Jaworski
G-AFCI	Short S.26	Buchan Marine Services
G-AFCL	Swallow 2	G. H. Forsaith
G-AFCR	Monarch	Air Schools
G-AFDT	Hornet Moth	Cardiff Aero Club
G-AFEA	Vega Gull	D. F. Little
G-AFEH	Vega Gull	Lancashire Aircraft Corp.
G-AFEN	Dragon Rapide	W. A. Rollason
G-AFEZ	Dragon Rapide	B.E.A.C.
G-AFFB	Dragon Rapide	Air Transport (Charter) (C.I.)
G-AFFD	Percival Q.6	R. H. Braime
G-AFFH	Taylor Cub	E. Brett
G-AFFJ	Piper Cub	Airways Aero Assoc.
G-AFGC	Swallow 2	H. Pain
G-AFGE	Swallow 2	G. C. Taylor
G-AFGH	Chilton D.W.I	J. M. Bickerton
G-AFGI	Chilton D. W.I	J. S. Sproule
G-AFGK	Whitney Straight	E. H. Thiery
G-AFGV	Swallow 2	I. H. Cameron
G-AFHC	Swallow 2	B. Arden
G-AFHH	Swallow 2	F. L. Haigh
G-AFHS	Swallow 2	J. Heath
G-AFIH	Dragon Rapide	Air Charter
G-AFIR	Luton Minor	A. W. Orde-Hume
G-AFJA	Watkinson Dingbat	
G-AFJB	Wicko	Miss M. Bennet
G-AFJC	Aeronca Chief	K. C. Millican
G-AFJO	Taylorcraft A	Rotol Flying Club
G-AFJP	Taylorcraft A	South Hants U.L.A.C.
G-AFJR	Tipsy Trainer	Tattersall's Garages
G-AFJS	Tipsy Trainer	Cardiff U.L.A.C.
G-AFJT	Tipsy Trainer	K. C. Millican
G-AFJU	Monarch	A. R. Pilgrim
G-AFKP	Tipsy Trainer	H. C. N. M. Oulton

Registration	Type	Owner or Operator
G-AFLT	Gemini 1A	Iliffe & Sons
G-AFLW	Monarch	Rolls-Royce Ltd.
G-AFMF	Dragon Rapide	J. W. Adamson
G-AFMJ	Dragon Rapide	Air Enterprises
G-AFMS	Moss M.A.2	W. H. Moss
G-AFNF	Moth Minor	E. I. H. Ward
G-AFNG	Moth Minor	S. J. Burt
G-AFNH	Moth Minor	G. S. Meek
G-AFNI	Moth Minor	H. W. J. Bethall
G-AFNJ	Moth Minor	J. Cooper
G-AFOB	Moth Minor	J. R. McConnell
G-AFOI	Dragon Rapide	Gibraltar Airways
G-AFOZ	Moth Minor	R.A.F. Flying Club
G-AFPD	Moth Minor	Airways Aero Assoc.
G-AFPH	Moth Minor	G. H. Forsaith
G-AFPM	Moth Minor	G. Whyte
G-AFPN	Moth Minor	J. N. & R. H. B. Enterprises
G-AFPO	Moth Minor	M. W. Woodard
G-AFPP	Piper Cub	W. Smyth
G-AFPR	Moth Minor	Miss J. L. Bird
G-AFRE	Hornet Moth	H. J. Aldington
G-AFRK	Dragon Rapide	B.E.A.C.
G-AFRR	Moth Minor	H. H. E. M. Winch
G-AFRU	Tipsy Trainer	L. D. Birkett
G-AFRV	Tipsy Trainer	J. H. Reed
G-AFRW	Gunton Special	R. Bracewell
G-AFRY	Moth Minor	G. S. Meek
G-AFSC	Tipsy Trainer	Mrs. E. F. Slade
G-AFSV	Chilton D.W.1A	A. R. Ward
G-AFSZ	J-4A Cub	Aero Hire
G-AFTA	Tom-tit	N. F. Duke
G-AFTN	Taylorcraft C.2	H. Pain
G-AFUA	Taylorcraft C	R. M. Smith
G-AFUB	Taylorcraft D	Southern Aircraft (Gatwick)
G-AFVN	Tipsy Trainer	I. H. Cameron
G-AFVR	Cygnet 2	T. F. W. Gunton
G-AFVT	Reliant	Fairey Aviation Co.
G-AFWM	Taylorcraft C.2	Earl of Cardigan
G-AFWO	Taylorcraft D	H. Sullivan
G-AFWS	J-4A Cub	S. Colley & Ptns.
G-AFWT	Tipsy Trainer	W. R. Trounson
G-AFXS	J-4A Cub	C. M. Newton
G-AFYH	Flamingo	British Air Transport
G-AFZI	Taylorcraft D	S. M. Cox
G-AFZP	Fokker F.22	Scottish Aviation
G-AFZY	Whitney Straight	Lord P. W. S. G. Calthorpe
G-AGAK	Hirtenberg H.S.9A	J. H. Davies
G-AGAX	Cygnet 2	L. V. Scarah
G-AGBD	Douglas DC-3	Skyways *Sky Hawk*
G-AGBG	Lockheed 14	North Sea Air Transport
G-AGBN	Cygnet 2	A. Costella
G-AGDL	Sparrowhawk	T. Shipside
G-AGDM	Dragon Rapide	Sivewright Airways
G-AGDP	Dragon Rapide	Modern Transport Ltd.
G-AGDT	Lockheed 12A	North Sea Air Transport
G-AGEE	Dragon Rapide	Gibraltar Airways
G-AGER	Sunderland 3	Aquila Airways
G-AGEU	Sunderland 3	Aquila Airways

Registration	Type	Owner or Operator
G-AGFU	Dragon Rapide	Air Charter Ltd.
G-AGHF	Dakota 3	North-West Airlines (I.o.M.)
G-AGHI	Dragon Rapide	C. L. Burton
G-AGHJ	Dakota 3	B.E.A.C.
G-AGHL	Dakota 3	B.E.A.C.
G-AGHM	Dakota 3	Skyways *Sky Monitor*
G-AGHO	Dakota 3	North-West Airlines (I.o.M.)
G-AGHP	Dakota 3	Field Aircraft Services
G-AGHS	Dakota 3	B.E.A.C.
G-AGIA	Sunderland 3	Aquila Airways
G-AGIF	Dragon Rapide	Ulster Aviation
G-AGIP	Dakota 3	B.E.A.C.
G-AGIS	Dakota 3	B.E.A.C.
G-AGIU	Dakota 3	B.E.A.C.
G-AGIW	Dakota 3	B.E.A.C.
G-AGIZ	Dakota 3	B.E.A.C.
G-AGJA	York I	B.O.A.C. *Kingston*
G-AGJB	York I	B.O.A.C. *Marathon*
G-AGJC	York I	B.O.A.C. *Malmesbury*
G-AGJD	York I	B.O.A.C. *Mansfield*
G-AGJE	York I	B.O.A.C. *Panama*
G-AGJG	Dragon Rapide	Mediterranean Air Services
G-AGJL	Sunderland 3	Aquila Airways
G-AGJP	Liberator	B.O.A.C.
G-AGJV	Dakota 3	B.E.A.C.
G-AGJW	Dakota 3	B.E.A.C.
G-AGJZ	Dakota 3	B.E.A.C.
G-AGKB	Dakota 4	B.O.A.C.
G-AGKC	Dakota 4	Airwork Ltd.
G-AGKV	Sunderland 3	Short Bros. & Harland
G-AGKW	Sunderland 3	Short Bros. & Harland
G-AGKX	Sandringham I	Aquila Airways
G-AGKY	Sunderland 3	Aquila Airways
G-AGLE	Dragon Rapide	C. L. Burton
G-AGLJ	Proctor 3	M.C.A.
G-AGLK	Auster 5	M.C.A.
G-AGLP	Dragon Rapide	C. L. Burton
G-AGLR	Dragon Rapide	Lees Hill Aviation
G-AGLS	Lancastrian I	B.O.A.C. *Nelson*
G-AGLW	Lancastrian I	B.O.A.C. *Northampton*
G-AGLY	Lancastrian I	B.O.A.C. *Norfolk*
G-AGMA	Lancastrian I	B.O.A.C. *Newport*
G-AGMG	Lancastrian I	B.O.A.C. *Nicosia*
G-AGMJ	Lancastrian I	B.O.A.C. *Naseby*
G-AGMK	Lancastrian I	B.O.A.C. *Newbury*
G-AGNG	Dakota 4	Eagle Aviation
G-AGNH	Dragon Rapide	M.C.A.
G-AGNK	Dakota 4	Sivewright Airways
G-AGNL	York I	B.O.A.C. *Mersey*
G-AGNM	York I	Eagle Aviation
G-AGNN	York I	B.O.A.C. *Atlantic Trader*
G-AGNO	York I	B.O.A.C. *Manton*
G-AGNP	York I	B.O.A.C. *Manchester*
G-AGNS	York I	B.O.A.C. *Pacific Trader*
G-AGNT	York I	B.O.A.C. *Mandalay*
G-AGNU	York I	B.O.A.C. *Nassau*
G-AGNV	York I	B.O.A.C. *Morville*
G-AGNW	York I	B.O.A.C. *Caribbean Trader*

Registration	Type	Owner or Operator
G–AGNX	York I	B.O.A.C. *Lima*
G–AGNY	York I	Eagle Aviation
G–AGNZ	York I	Eagle Aviation
G–AGOA	York I	B.O.A.C. *Montrose*
G–AGOB	York I	B.O.A.C. *Milford*
G–AGOD	York I	B.O.A.C. *Midlothian*
G–AGOE	York I	B.O.A.C. *Medway*
G–AGOF	York I	B.O.A.C. *McDuff*
G–AGOG	Proctor 3	M.C.A.
G–AGOH	Autocrat	Blackburn Aircraft
G–AGOJ	Dragon Rapide	Lancashire Aircraft Corp.
G–AGOR	Dragon Rapide	Iraq Petroleum Transport Co.
G–AGOS	Desford	Reid & Sigrist
G–AGOY	Messenger 3	Uniformity Shoes
G–AGPB	Avro 19	M.C.A.
G–AGPG	Avro 19	A. V. Roe & Co.
G–AGPH	Dragon Rapide	B.E.A.C.
G–AGPJ	Dove	M.o.S.
G–AGPU	Avro 19	Secretary of State for Air
G–AGPW	Brabazon I	M.o.S.
G–AGPX	Messenger 3	North Sea Air Transport Ltd.
G–AGRA	Tiger Moth	M.C.A.
G–AGRB	Tiger Moth	M.C.A.
G–AGRC	Tudor 4C	M.o.S. *Star Troilus*
G–AGRD	Tudor I	M.o.S. *Star Cymbeline*
G–AGRF	Tudor 4B	M.o.S. *Elizabeth of England*
G–AGRG	Tudor 4C	M.o.S. *Star Cresida*
G–AGRH	Tudor Freighter I	M.C.A. *Star Ceres*
G–AGRI	Tudor 4C	M.C.A. *Star Oberon*
G–AGRJ	Tudor Freighter I	M.C.A. *Star Celia*
G–AGRK	Tudor 4C	M.o.S. *Star Prospero*
G–AGRL	Tudor 4C	M.o.S. *Star Proteus*
G–AGRP	Viking IA	Sale & Co.
G–AGRR	Viking IA	M.o.S.
G–AGRV	Viking IA	Sale & Co.
G–AGRW	Viking IA	Sale & Co.
G–AGRY	Tudor 2	D. C. T. Bennett
G–AGSH	Dragon Rapide	B.E.A.C.
G–AGSI	Dragon Rapide	Olley Air Service
G–AGSK	Dragon Rapide	B.E.A.C.
G–AGSL	York I	B.O.A.C. *Morley*
G–AGSM	York I	B.O.A.C. *Malvern*
G–AGSN	York I	B.O.A.C. *Marlow*
G–AGSO	York I	B.O.A.C. *Manston*
G–AGSP	York I	B.O.A.C. *Santiago*
G–AGSR	Be 550 Bibi	H. Clive-Smith
G–AGSV	Avro 711A	M.o.S.
G–AGSX	Proctor 5	Hunting Air Travel
G–AGTC	Proctor 5	Percival Aircraft
G–AGTE	Proctor 5	Butlin's Ltd.
G–AGTF	Proctor 5	Cambridge University Gliding Club
G–AGTG	Aerocar	Portsmouth Aviation
G–AGTH	Proctor 3	B.O.A.C. *Star Pixie*
G–AGTL	Lockheed 12A	F. S. Cotton
G–AGTM	Dragon Rapide	Iraq Petroleum Transport Co.
G–AGTN	Dragon Rapide	Iraq Petroleum Transport Co.
G–AGTO	Autocrat	T. W. Shipside
G–AGTP	Autocrat	T. Carlyle

Registration	Type	Owner or Operator
G-AGTR	Autocrat	R. H. Braime
G-AGTT	Autocrat	Inter-City Air Services
G-AGTV	Autocrat	G. S. Pine
G-AGTW	Autocrat	Anglo-Continental Air Services
G-AGTX	Autocrat	W. Nadin
G-AGTY	Autocrat	T. Shipside Ltd.
G-AGUA	Ambassador	M.o.S.
G-AGUB	Hermes 2	M.o.S.
G-AGUD	Avro 19	M.C.A.
G-AGUF	Dragon Rapide	J. A. R. Helps
G-AGUG	Dragon Rapide	Lancashire Aircraft Corp.
G-AGUH	Avro 19	Hawker Aircraft
G-AGUP	Dragon Rapide	B.E.A.C.
G-AGUR	Dragon Rapide	B.E.A.C.
G-AGUS	Gemini 2	Walter Instruments
G-AGUU	Dragon Rapide	B.E.A.C.
G-AGUV	Dragon Rapide	B.E.A.C.
G-AGUX	Avro 19	Fairey Aviation Co.
G-AGVA	Avro 19	M.C.A.
G-AGVB	Wayfarer 21	Bowmaker Ltd.
G-AGVC	Freighter 21	Bristol Aeroplane Co.
G-AGVD	Shetland 2	M.o.S.
G-AGVF	Autocrat	Loxhams Flying Service
G-AGVG	Autocrat	R. W. Braime
G-AGVH	Autocrat	R. W. Kerry
G-AGVI	Autocrat	Bidgood & Catton Taxi-Planes
G-AGVJ	Autocrat	British Air Transport
G-AGVK	Autocrat	M. C. D. Wilson
G-AGVL	Autocrat	Bembridge and Sandown Aero Club
G-AGVM	Autocrat	Bristol & Wessex Aero Club
G-AGVN	Autocrat	R. A. Walley
G-AGVO	Autocrat	E. L. Sprayson
G-AGVP	Autocrat	Wiltshire School of Flying
G-AGVR	Autocrat	British Salmson Aero Engines
G-AGVU	Autocrat	J. H. Watts
G-AGVX	Mercury 4	W. S. Shackleton
G-AGVZ	Lockheed 12A	
G-AGWA	Avro 19	M.C.A.
G-AGWB	Proctor 3	Secretary of State for Air
G-AGWC	Dragon Rapide	Air Transport (Charter) (C.I.)
G-AGWE	Avro 19	M.C.A.
G-AGWF	Avro 19/1	M.C.A.
G-AGWI	Lancastrian 3	Flight Refuelling
G-AGWL	Lancastrian 3	Flight Refuelling
G-AGWN	Lockheed 12A	Skyways Ltd.
G-AGWP	Dragon Rapide	Morton Air Services
G-AGWR	Dragon Rapide	Morton Air Services
G-AGWS	Dakota	Scottish Aviation
G-AGWT	Nighthawk	R. Crewdson
G-AGWV	Proctor 1	G. M. Tonge
G-AGWY	Autocrat	T. Carlyle
G-AGXB	Autocrat	Lt. Col. J. J. Dykes
G-AGXC	Autocrat	D. H. Eastwood
G-AGXD	Autocrat	Lancashire Aircraft Corp.
G-AGXF	Autocrat	H. Mitchell
G-AGXG	Autocrat	A. J. Linnel
G-AGXH	Autocrat	Hunting Aerosurveys
G-AGXJ	Autocrat	United Services Flying Club
G-AGXK	Autocrat	Midland Aero Club

Registration	Type	Owner or Operator
G–AGXM	Autocrat	R. G. Parker
G–AGXN	Autocrat	G. Brady
G–AGXO	Autocrat	S. W. Freestone
G–AGXP	Autocrat	Private Flying (Ipswich) Ltd.
G–AGXS	Autocrat	M. A. Crouch
G–AGXT	Autocrat	United Services Flying Club
G–AGXU	Autocrat	Fairey Aviation Co.
G–AGXV	Autocrat	R. G. Presland, W. H. Wetton
G–AGXX	Autocrat	Marshalls' Flying Schools
G–AGYA	Proctor I	R. J. Jones
G–AGYB	Proctor I	J. Drennan
G–AGYC	Proctor I	W. A. Rollason
G–AGYD	Autocrat	J. C. H. Wildbore
G–AGYF	Autocrat	Hastings & East Sussex Air Service
G–AGYH	Autocrat	Coventry (Civil) Aviation
G–AGYI	Autocrat	Royal Artillery Aero Club
G–AGYJ	Autocrat	R. G. Banks
G–AGYK	Autocrat	R. J. Bowes
G–AGYL	Autocrat	W. A. Munro
G–AGYM	Autocrat	W. M. B. May
G–AGYN	Autocrat	London Aero Club
G–AGYO	Autocrat	Airways Aero Assoc.
G–AGYP	Autocrat	J. L. Shaw
G–AGYR	Autocrat	R. P. Alder
G–AGYT	Autocrat	J. H. Watts
G–AGYU	Autocrat	Marshalls' Flying Schools
G–AGYX	Dakota 3	B.E.A.C.
G–AGYZ	Dakota 3	B.E.A.C.
G–AGZB	Dakota 3	B.E.A.C.
G–AGZC	Dakota 3	B.E.A.C.
G–AGZD	Dakota 3	B.E.A.C.
G–AGZF	Dakota 3	Scottish Aviation Ltd.
G–AGZG	Dakota 3	Scottish Aviation Ltd.
G–AGZJ	Dragon Rapide	J. H. Watts
G–AGZK	Dragon Rapide	Iraq Petroleum Co., Ltd.
G–AGZM	Proctor I	Herts & Essex Aero Club
G–AGZO	Dragon Rapide	Marshalls' Flying Schools
G–AGZS	Avro 19	M.C.A.
G–AGZT	Avro 19	M.C.A.
G–AGZU	Dragon Rapide	Herts & Essex Aero Club
G–AGZW	Voyager	Southampton Air Services
G–AHAA	Mercury 6	K. E. Millard & Co., Ltd.
G–AHAB	Proctor I	C. E. Berens
G–AHAC	Envoy 3	Private Charter Ltd.
G–AHAD	Taylorcraft D	A. Rees
G–AHAE	Taylorcraft D	Newcastle-on-Tyne Aero Club
G–AHAG	Dragon Rapide	North Sea Air Transport
G–AHAI	Taylorcraft D	Denham Flying Club
G–AHAK	Taylorcraft D	Air Taxis (Croydon)
G–AHAL	Autocrat	A. Christian
G–AHAM	Autocrat	T. E. Dalton
G–AHAO	Autocrat	Air Schools
G–AHAP	Autocrat	Kennings Ltd.
G–AHAR	Autocrat	A. M. Ashery
G–AHAT	Autocrat	Congo Charter Air Services
G–AHAU	Autocrat	Col. C. W. D. Rowe
G–AHAV	Autocrat	J. S. Bancroft
G–AHAW	Autocrat	Lawson's Aerial Photographs

Registration	Type	Owner or Operator
G-AHAX	Autocrat	J. D. H. Radford
G-AHAY	Autocrat	Fairey Aviation Co.
G-AHBA	Proctor 5	Dunlop Rubber Co.
G-AHBC	Proctor 5	Donaldson Bros.
G-AHBD	Proctor 5	Sir W. G. Armstrong-Whitworth Aircraft
G-AHBH	Proctor 5	Western Airways
G-AHBI	Proctor 5	Goodhew Aviation Co.
G-AHBJ	Proctor 5	Yellow Air Taxis
G-AHBL	Hornet Moth	West London Aero Club
G-AHBM	Hornet Moth	West London Aero Club
G-AHBO	Taylorcraft D	H. E. Scrope
G-AHBS	Proctor I	L. H. B. Roper
G-AHBT	Lancastrian 3	Skyways *Sky Ranger*
G-AHBV	Lancastrian 3	Skyways
G-AHCC	Lancastrian 3	Skyways *Sky Chieftain*
G-AHCG	Taylorcraft D	Boston Air Transport
G-AHCI	Taylorcraft D	Brooklands Aviation
G-AHCK	Autocrat	British Air Transport
G-AHCL	Autocrat	United Services Flying Club
G-AHCM	Autocrat	G. & A. Morgan Trust
G-AHCN	Autocrat	Bristol & Wessex Aero Club
G-AHCO	Autocrat	Lockwood's Flying Services
G-AHCR	Taylorcraft D	Wiltshire School of Flying
G-AHCT	Dakota 3	B.E.A.C.
G-AHCU	Dakota 3	B.E.A.C.
G-AHCV	Dakota 3	B.E.A.C.
G-AHCX	Dakota 3	B.E.A.C.
G-AHCZ	Dakota 3	B.E.A.C.
G-AHDD	Tiger Moth	Wiltshire School of Flying
G-AHDH	Proctor I	Newman Aircraft
G-AHDI	Proctor I	S. Caliendi
G-AHDJ	Proctor I	Newman Aircraft
G-AHDM	Halton I	Westminster Airways
G-AHDN	Halton I	Aviation Traders
G-AHDO	Halton I	Bond Air Services
G-AHDS	Halton I	Bond Air Services
G-AHDU	Halton I	Aviation Traders
G-AHDV	Halton I	Westminster Airways
G-AHDW	Halton I	Aviation Traders
G-AHDY	Liberator 3	Scottish Aviation
G-AHDZ	Oxford 2	Scottish Aviation
G-AHEA	Dragon Rapide	Lancashire Aircraft Corp.
G-AHED	Dragon Rapide	Marshall's Flying School
G-AHEE	Proctor I	Hunting Flying Clubs
G-AHEF	Consul	Airspeed Ltd.
G-AHEH	Consul	G. C. S. Pearson
G-AHEI	Taylorcraft D	R.A.F. Flying Club
G-AHEJ	Constellation	B.O.A.C. *Bristol II*
G-AHEK	Constellation	B.O.A.C. *Berwick II*
G-AHEL	Constellation	B.O.A.C. *Bangor II*
G-AHEM	Constellation	B.O.A.C. *Balmoral*
G-AHEN	Constellation	B.O.A.C. *Baltimore*
G-AHER	Sunderland 3	Aquila Airways
G-AHES	Proctor I	Silver City Airways
G-AHET	Vega Gull	Essex Aero Ltd.
G-AHEU	Proctor I	J. H. Watts
G-AHEV	Proctor I	J. H. Watts

Registration	Type	Owner or Operator
G-AHEY	York	B.O.A.C. *Star Quest*
G-AHFA	York	B.O.A.C. *Star Dale*
G-AHFB	York	B.O.A.C. *Star Stream*
G-AHFC	York	B.O.A.C. *Star Dew*
G-AHFD	York	B.O.A.C. *Star Mist*
G-AHFE	York	B.O.A.C. *Star Vista*
G-AHFF	York	B.O.A.C. *Star Gleam*
G-AHFG	York	B.O.A.C. *Star Haze*
G-AHFH	York	B.O.A.C. *Star Glitter*
G-AHFK	Proctor 3	Kelvin & Hughes
G-AHFL	Walrus I	United Whalers
G-AHFM	Walrus I	United Whalers
G-AHFN	Walrus I	C. Mauritzen Ltd.
G-AHFO	Walrus I	United Whalers
G-AHFP	Messenger 4	Airwork
G-AHFR	Proctor 5	Rolls-Royce Ltd.
G-AHFS	Consul	British Air Transport
G-AHFT	Consul	Morton Air Services
G-AHFU	Proctor I	Chartair
G-AHFW	Proctor I	S. G. Newport
G-AHFY	Proctor I	L. G. S. Payne
G-AHGA	Proctor I	Stewart Smith & Co.
G-AHGC	Dragon Rapide	Hawker Aircraft
G-AHGD	Dragon Rapide	North Sea Air Transport
G-AHGF	Dragon Rapide	F. A. Hill
G-AHGG	Dragon Rapide	Olley Air Service
G-AHGH	Dragon Rapide	Patrick Motors
G-AHGI	Dragon Rapide	Patrick Motors
G-AHGJ	Proctor 5	B. N. White & Spencer Ltd.
G-AHGL	Proctor 5	E. S. Davis
G-AHGM	Proctor 5	Hunting Air Travel
G-AHGN	Proctor 5	M.C.A.
G-AHGR	Proctor 5	D. J. Bennett
G-AHGS	Proctor 5	Patrick Motors
G-AHGT	Proctor 5	Helliwells
G-AHGU	Oxford	Bristol Aeroplane Co.
G-AHGX	Taylorcraft D	Wiltshire School of Flying
G-AHGY	Taylorcraft D	Wycombe Flying Club
G-AHGZ	Taylorcraft D	Carlight Trailers
G-AHHB	Taylorcraft D	Light Planes (Lancs.)
G-AHHC	Taylorcraft D	Inter-City Airways
G-AHHH	Autocrat	Anglo-Continental Air Services
G-AHHK	Autocrat	J. M. S. Chipperfield
G-AHHL	Autocrat	Yellow Air Taxis
G-AHHM	Autocrat	Weston Webb
G-AHHN	Autocrat	F. B. Austin
G-AHHO	Autocrat	G. S. Pine
G-AHHP	Autocrat	E. E. Kimbell
G-AHHR	Autocrat	M. W. B. May
G-AHHS	Autocrat	G. G. Plank & Co.
G-AHHT	Autocrat	F. H. W. Wheaton
G-AHHU	Autocrat	Colt Ventilation
G-AHHW	Autocrat	J. C. Hoyland
G-AHHX	Autocrat	Light Planes (Lancs.)
G-AHHY	Taylorcraft D	Sivewright Airways
G-AHHZ	Taylorcraft D	G. C. Mawer
G-AHIA	Dragon Rapide	Skyways
G-AHIB	Avro 19	Thorne Aviation

Registration	Type	Owner or Operator
G-AHIC	Avro 19	M.C.A.
G-AHID	Avro 19	M.C.A.
G-AHIE	Avro 19	Thorne Aviation
G-AHIF	Avro 19	F. A. Laker
G-AHIG	Avro 19	M.C.A.
G-AHIH	Avro 19	M.C.A.
G-AHII	Avro 19	Starways
G-AHIJ	Avro 19	M.C.A.
G-AHIK	Avro 19	Starways
G-AHIL	Solent 2	M.C.A. *City of Salisbury*
G-AHIM	Solent 2	M.C.A. *Scarborough*
G-AHIN	Solent 2	M.C.A. *Southampton*
G-AHIO	Solent 2	M.C.A. *Somerset*
G-AHIR	Solent 2	M.C.A. *Sark*
G-AHIS	Solent 2	M.C.A. *City of York*
G-AHIT	Solent 2	M.C.A. *Severn*
G-AHIU	Solent 2	M.C.A. *Solway*
G-AHIV	Solent 2	M.C.A. *Salcombe*
G-AHIW	Solent 2	M.C.A. *Stornoway*
G-AHIY	Solent 2	M.C.A. *Southsea*
G-AHIZ	Tiger Moth	London Aero Club
G-AHJA	Dragon Rapide	Vickers-Armstrongs Ltd.
G-AHJD	Wayfarer 21	Airwork
G-AHJS	Dragon Rapide	Fairey Aviation Co.
G-AHJU	Lancaster 1	Flight Refuelling
G-AHJX	Consul	Morton Air Services
G-AHJY	Consul	N. H. Teakle
G-AHJZ	Consul	De Havilland Aircraft Co.
G-AHKA	Dragon Rapide	De Havilland Aircraft Co.
G-AHKB	Dragon Rapide	Vickers-Armstrongs Ltd.
G-AHKH	Anson 1	British Air Transport
G-AHKK	Halifax 8	
G-AHKL	Gemini 1A	Smithfield Refrigerator Co.
G-AHKO	Taylorcraft D	F. R. J. Britten
G-AHKP	Hawk Trainer 3	Wiltshire School of Flying
G-AHKS	Dragon Rapide	B.E.A.C.
G-AHKT	Dragon Rapide	B.E.A.C.
G-AHKU	Dragon Rapide	B.E.A.C.
G-AHKV	Dragon Rapide	B.E.A.C.
G-AHKX	Avro 19	Smiths Aircraft Instruments
G-AHKY	Miles M.18/2	H. B. Iles
G-AHKZ	Tiger Moth	Coventry (Civil) Aviation
G-AHLA	Tiger Moth	Helliwells Ltd.
G-AHLB	Tiger Moth	Midland Bank Flying Club
G-AHLD	Tiger Moth	Midland Bank Flying Club
G-AHLF	Dragon Rapide	Westland Aircraft
G-AHLH	Lockheed 12A	Earl of Granard
G-AHLI	Auster 3	Vickers-Armstrongs Ltd.
G-AHLJ	Taylorcraft Plus D	Vickers-Armstrongs Ltd.
G-AHLK	Auster 3	Vickers-Armstrongs Ltd.
G-AHLL	Dragon Rapide	B.E.A.C.
G-AHLM	Dragon Rapide	Marshall's Flying School
G-AHLN	Dragon Rapide	Ulster Aviation
G-AHLO	Puss Moth	Autowork (Winchester)
G-AHLR	Tiger Moth	Goodhew Aviation
G-AHLT	Tiger Moth	Walker & Thompson
G-AHLV	York 1	Skyways *Sky Courier*
G-AHMD	Consul	Lancashire Aircraft Corp.

Registration	Type	Owner or Operator
G–AHME	Tiger Moth	J. W. Tomkins
G–AHML	Tiger Moth	Brooklands Aviation
G–AHMM	Tiger Moth	Brooklands Aviation
G–AHMN	Tiger Moth	Brooklands Aviation
G–AHMP	Proctor I	de Havilland Engine Co.
G–AHMR	Proctor I	Barnet Instruments
G–AHMT	Proctor I	Scottish Aviation
G–AHMV	Proctor I	Field Aircraft Services
G–AHNA	Proctor I	A. S. K. Paine
G–AHNB	Proctor 2	Cinque Ports Flying Club
G–AHNC	Tiger Moth	Light Planes (Lancs.)
G–AHND	Tiger Moth	Air Navigation and Trading Co.
G–AHNE	Hawk Trainer 3	Air Navigation and Trading Co.
G–AHNG	Taylorcraft D	T. J. S. Kidner
G–AHNH	Tudor 4C	M.o.S. *Star Ophelia*
G–AHNI	Tudor Freighter 4B	M.C.A. *Star Olivia*
G–AHNJ	Tudor 4	B.O.A.C. *Star Lion*
G–AHNK	Tudor 4	B.O.A.C. *Star Panther*
G–AHNL	Tudor Freighter 4B	M.C.A.
G–AHNM	Tudor Freighter 4B	M.C.A. *Star Cluster*
G–AHNN	Tudor 4	B.O.A.C. *Star Leopard*
G–AHNO	Tudor 4B	M.C.A. *Star Titania*
G–AHNR	Tudor 4C	M.o.S. *Star Theseus*
G–AHNS	Anson I	Air Service Training
G–AHNT	Anson I	Air Service Training
G–AHNU	Hawk Trainer 3	Wolverhampton Flying School
G–AHNV	Hawk Trainer 3	Wolverhampton Flying School
G–AHNW	Hawk Trainer 3	H. T. Ryan
G–AHNZ	Taylorcraft D	A. Walmesley
G–AHOB	Master 2	
G–AHOM	Percival Q/6	Ductile Steels
G–AHON	Viking IA	A. J. Gaul
G–AHOP	Viking IA	British Nederland Airservices
G–AHOR	Viking IA	Sale & Co.
G–AHOT	Viking IA	A. J. Gaul
G–AHOV	Viking IA	Sale & Co.
G–AHOW	Viking IA	Sale & Co.
G–AHOY	Viking I	Hunting Air Travel
G–AHPB	Viking I	Hunting Air Travel
G–AHPC	Viking I	Hunting Air Travel
G–AHPD	Viking I	Hunting Air Travel
G–AHPH	Viking IA	B.E.A.C.
G–AHPI	Viking IA	Hunting Air Travel
G–AHPJ	Viking IA	Hunting Air Travel
G–AHPL	Viking IB	B.E.A.C. *Verdant*
G–AHPM	Viking IB	B.E.A.C. *Verderer*
G–AHPN	Viking IB	B.E.A.C. *Ventnor*
G–AHPO	Viking IB	B.E.A.C. *Venture*
G–AHPP	Viking IB	B.E.A.C. *Venus*
G–AHPR	Viking IB	B.E.A.C. *Verily*
G–AHPS	Viking IB	B.E.A.C. *Verity*
G–AHPT	Dragon Rapide	Island Air Charters
G–AHPU	Dragon Rapide 2	J. E. Steel
G–AHRB	Dove I	Skyways *Sky Maid*
G–AHRC	Tiger Moth	J. C. Rice
G–AHRF	Viscount	M.o.S.
G–AHRG	Viscount	M.o.S.

Registration	Type	Owner or Operator
G-AHRH	Dragon Rapide	Gloster Aircraft Co.
G-AHRI	Dove	Iraq Petroleum Transport Co.
G-AHRK	Consul	Silver City Airways
G-AHRL	Tiger Moth	Blackburn Aircraft Co.
G-AHRM	Tiger Moth	Blackburn & General Aircraft
G-AHRN	Tiger Moth	Blackburn & General Aircraft
G-AHRR	Tiger Moth	Inter City Airways
G-AHRV	Tiger Moth	E. S. Morrell
G-AHRX	Tiger Moth	Goodhew Aviation Co.
G-AHRY	Proctor 3	Hunting Aerosurveys
G-AHSA	Tutor	J. Neasham
G-AHSB	Taylorcraft D	W. Greenlalgh
G-AHSD	Taylorcraft D	Lockwood's Flying Services
G-AHSG	Taylorcraft D	A. R. Julian
G-AHSH	Autocrat	R. A. Young
G-AHSI	Autocrat	Longford Engineering Co.
G-AHSJ	Taylorcraft D	J. S. Swansea
G-AHSK	Taylorcraft D	I. H. Cameron
G-AHSM	Autocrat	A. J. Pickering
G-AHSN	Autocrat	R.N. Flying Club
G-AHSO	Autocrat	Universal Flying Services
G-AHSP	Autocrat	J. G. Robertson & Co.
G-AHSR	Autocrat	R. W. Ward
G-AHSS	Autocrat	Loxham's Flying Services
G-AHST	Autocrat	D. Everall
G-AHSW	Autocrat	C. G. Wheatley
G-AHSX	Autocrat	Barton Motors (Preston)
G-AHTE	Proctor 5	C. G. Wheatley
G-AHTF	Proctor 5	Western Airways
G-AHTG	Proctor 5	Dawn Hire
G-AHTI	Proctor 5	Fairway Engineering Co.
G-AHTK	Proctor 5	Willis Hole Aviation
G-AHTL	Proctor 5	Dennis Aviation
G-AHTM	Proctor 5	P. M. Bennett & Co.
G-AHTN	Proctor I	Aerial Medical Service
G-AHTR	Dragon Rapide	Anglo-Iranian Oil Co.
G-AHTT	Dragon Rapide	Anglo-Iranian Oil Co.
G-AHTV	Proctor I	Air Service Training
G-AHTW	Oxford I	Boulton Paul Aircraft
G-AHTX	Aerovan 3	S. G. Newport
G-AHTY	Dragon Rapide	North Sea Air Transport
G-AHTZ	Cierva C.30A	Rota Towels
G-AHUB	Tiger Moth	London Aero Club
G-AHUE	Tiger Moth	Airwork
G-AHUG	Taylorcraft D	G. F. K. Donaldsoh
G-AHUI	Messenger 2A	Derek Crouch (Contractors)
G-AHUJ	Hawk Trainer 3	J. McDonald & Sons
G-AHUL	Hawk Trainer 3	Home Counties Aero Club
G-AHUM	Taylorcraft D	T. H. Marshall
G-AHUN	Tiger Moth	Hampshire School of Flying
G-AHUO	Tiger Moth	Hampshire School of Flying
G-AHUT	Tiger Moth	Universal Flying Services
G-AHUU	Globe Swift	Helliwells Ltd.
G-AHUV	Tiger Moth	Airwork
G-AHUX	Proctor I	J. Oliver
G-AHUZ	Proctor I	N. W. Charlton

Registration	Type	Owner or Operator
G-AHVA	Proctor I	Extractors (Hull)
G-AHVB	Proctor I	Air Couriers
G-AHVC	Proctor I	Air Couriers
G-AHVG	Proctor I	Blackburn & General Aircraft
G-AHVK	Proctor I	Air Kruise (Kent)
G-AHVN	Lancaster I	Flight Refuelling
G-AHVO	Avro 626	A. G. Harding
G-AHVP	Taylorcraft D	Midland Aero Club
G-AHVR	Taylorcraft D	Midland Aero Club
G-AHVS	Taylorcraft D	Midland Aero Club
G-AHVU	Tiger Moth	Cardiff Aero Club
G-AHVV	Tiger Moth	Plymouth & District Aero Club
G-AHVW	Tiger Moth	J. MacDonald & Sons
G-AHVX	Tiger Moth	Air Service Training
G-AHVY	Tiger Moth	Air Service Training
G-AHWA	Tiger Moth	Air Service Training
G-AHWB	Tiger Moth	Air Service Training
G-AHWC	Tiger Moth	Air Service Training
G-AHWD	Taylorcraft D	Newcastle-upon-Tyne Aero Club
G-AHWE	Tiger Moth	Weston Aero Club
G-AHWF	Dragon Rapide	Iraq Petroleum Transport Co.
G-AHWH	Globe Swift	C. G. Wheatley
G-AHWI	Taylorcraft D	Bristol & Wessex Aero Club
G-AHWJ	Taylorcraft D	Bristol & Wessex Aero Club
G-AHWK	Taylorcraft D	Bristol & Wessex Aero Club
G-AHWN	Halifax 8	Lancashire Aircraft Corp.
G-AHWO	Proctor 5	Gerald C. Judd Ltd.
G-AHWR	Proctor 5	North Sea Air Transport
G-AHWS	Proctor 5	Yorkshire Aeroplane Club
G-AHWT	Proctor 5	L. M. Cooper
G-AHWU	Proctor 5	Shell Refining & Marketing Co.
G-AHWV	Proctor 5	D. Napier & Sons
G-AHWW	Proctor 5	A. J. Bradshaw
G-AHWZ	Proctor 5	Colnbrook Trading Co.
G-AHXB	Tiger Moth	London Aero Club
G-AHXC	Tiger Moth	London Aero Club
G-AHXE	Taylorcraft D	R. A. McMurtrie
G-AHXF	Taylorcraft D	W. S. Shackleton
G-AHXG	Taylorcraft D	H. W. Ayre
G-AHXH	Aerovan 4	S. G. Newport
G-AHXI	Cierva C.30A	Southern Aircraft (Gatwick)
G-AHXK	Avro 19	Sivewright Airways
G-AHXL	Avro 19	B.E.A.C.
G-AHXM	Avro 19	B.E.A.C.
G-AHXN	Tiger Moth	Marshall's Flying School
G-AHXR	Messenger 2A	Hon. J. B. Fermor-Hesketh
G-AHXS	Anson I	Fairey Aviation Co.
G-AHXU	Marathon 2	M.o.S.
G-AHXW	Dragon Rapide	B.E.A.C.
G-AHXX	Dragon Rapide	B.E.A.C.
G-AHXZ	Dragon Rapide	B.E.A.C.
G-AHYB	Liberator	B.O.A.C.
G-AHYD	Liberator	B.O.A.C.
G-AHYF	Liberator	B.O.A.C.
G-AHYG	Liberator	B.O.A.C.
G-AHYL	Hawk Trainer 3	Fairey Aviation Co.
G-AHYM	Hawk Trainer 3	Fairey Aviation Co.
G-AHYN	Avro 19	Sivewright Airways

Above : Boeing STRATO-CRUISER. Biggest air liner in regular service. Operated into London Airport by B.O.A.C., P.A.A. and A.O.A.

Right : Bristol BRABA-ZON I. Designed to fly direct from London to New York with 100 passengers. G–AGPW has eight Centaurus piston-engines. Brabazon 2 (G–AIML) will have eight Proteus "propjets."

Below : Douglas DC–6. Successor to the famous Dakota and Skymaster, the DC–6 is here seen in S.A.S. markings.

Left: Avro YORK. Developed from the Lancaster bomber and mainstay of the R.A.F.'s contribution to the Berlin Air Lift in 1948–9. (*F.A.M.A. photo.*)

Above : Lockheed CONSTELLATION. More than 210 "Connies" are in service with 14 major world airlines. VT-DAR is flown between Bombay and London by Air India International.

Left : Canadair DC-4M2. The Canadair Four, 22 of which constitute B.O.A.C.'s *Argonaut* Class, is a Canadian-built development of the DC-4 with Merlin engines and DC-6 type cabin pressurisation. The aircraft illustrated is one of T.C.A.'s 20 *North Stars.*

Registration	Type	Owner or Operator
G–AHYP	Tiger Moth	Aikman Airways
G–AHYY	Sandringham 5	B.O.A.C. *Portsmouth*
G–AHZA	Sandringham 5	B.O.A.C. *Penzance*
G–AHZC	Sandringham 5	B.O.A.C. *Pembroke*
G–AHZD	Sandringham 5	B.O.A.C. *Portmarnock*
G–AHZE	Sandringham 5	B.O.A.C. *Portsea*
G–AHZF	Sandringham 5	B.O.A.C. *Poole*
G–AHZG	Sandringham 5	B.O.A.C. *Pevensey*
G–AHZH	Tiger Moth	Hampshire School of Flying
G–AHZS	Messenger 2A	H. C. Kennard
G–AHZT	Messenger 2A	H. Deterding
G–AHZU	Messenger 2A	Tractor Spares Ltd.
G–AHZV	Consul	Lancashire Aircraft Corp.
G–AHZW	Consul	Lancashire Aircraft Corp.
G–AHZY	Proctor 5	Anglo-American Oil Co.
G–AIAA	Proctor 5	T. Wayman-Hales
G–AIAE	Proctor 5	A. G. D. Mackenzie
G–AIAF	Proctor 5	T. W. Dupree
G–AIAG	Proctor 5	W. J. Twitchell
G–AIAH	Consul	Morton Air Services
G–AIAI	Hawk Trainer	Airways Aero Assoc.
G–AIAJ	Messenger 2A	Major Hubert Blount
G–AIAP	Halifax 8	Eagle Aviation
G–AIAR	Halifax 8	Chartair
G–AIAT	Oxford I	B.O.A.C.
G–AIAU	Oxford I	B.O.A.C.
G–AIAV	Oxford I	B.O.A.C.
G–AIAW	Oxford I	B.O.A.C.
G–AIAX	Oxford I	B.O.A.C.
G–AIBB	Dragon Rapide	Patrick Motors
G–AIBC	Consul	F. C. Wilmer
G–AIBD	Messenger 2A	T. Carlyle
G–AIBE	Fulmar 2	Fairey Aviation Co.
G–AIBF	Consul	Silver City Airways
G–AIBH	Autocrat	M. M. Mallorie
G–AIBL	Autocrat	Machine Tools Ltd.
G–AIBM	Autocrat	Mr. & Mrs. R. E. O. Velten
G–AIBN	Tiger Moth	Marshall's Flying School
G–AIBP	Autocrat	P. O. Bennie
G–AIBR	Autocrat	Brooklands Aviation
G–AIBS	Autocrat	G. & A. Morgan Trust
G–AIBT	Autocrat	Sykes & Robinson
G–AIBW	Autocrat	Air Schools
G–AIBX	Autocrat	East Riding Flying Club
G–AIBY	Autocrat	J. D. H. Radford
G–AIBZ	Autocrat	Wright Aviation
G–AICA	Arrow	Auster Aircraft
G–AICD	Hawk Trainer 3	Bournemouth Flying Club
G–AICE	Hawk Trainer 3	Bournemouth Flying Club
G–AICM	Freighter I	M.C.A. (Hunting Aerosurveys)
G–AICT	Wayfarer 2A	Bristol Aeroplane Co.
G–AICY	Dove I	Iraq Petroleum Transport Co.
G–AIDB	Tiger Moth	Wiltshire School of Flying
G–AIDD	Tiger Moth	Brooklands Aviation
G–AIDE	Monarch	B. G. Heron
G–AIDF	Hawk Trainer	Hunting Flying Club
G–AIDH	Messenger 2A	Mrs. L. K. King
G–AIDI	Aerovan 3	S. G. Newport

Registration	Type	Owner or Operator
G AIDK	Messenger 2A	Wallis & Linnell
G AIDL	Tiger Moth	E. C. Gander-Dower
G AIDN	Spitfire Tr. 8	Vickers-Armstrongs
G-AIDO	Gemini 1A	E. G. Hayes
G-AIDR	Tiger Moth	Herts & Essex Aero Club
G-AIDS	Tiger Moth	Herts & Essex Aero Club
G-AIDT	Tiger Moth	Herts & Essex Aero Club
G-AIDV	Tiger Moth	Herts & Essex Aero Club
G-AIDW	Consul	Dexford Motors
G-AIDX	Consul	Anglo-American Oil Co.
G-AIDZ	Consul	British Air Transport
G-AIEA	Consul	British Air Transport
G-AIEB	Proctor 1	W./Cdr. R. L. Bowes
G-AIED	Proctor 1	Shell Mex & B.P.
G-AIEE	Proctor 1	P. Lennox
G-AIEG	Proctor 2	W. Graham & M. J. Edwards
G-AIEH	Proctor 2	R. F. Martin
G-AIEK	Messenger 2A	A. J. Linnell
G-AIEL	Tiger Moth	R. H. Braime
G-AIEN	Proctor 5	Kearsley Airways
G-AIEP	Proctor 5	Hornton Airways
G-AIER	Proctor 5	Blue Line Airways
G-AIES	Proctor 5	D. H. L. McCowen
G-AIET	Proctor 5	Vivian Van Damm
G-AIEV	Proctor 5	N. King
G-AIEX	Proctor 1	Yorkshire Aeroplane Club
G-AIEY	Proctor 1	Vosper Ltd.
G-AIFD	Anson 1	Straight Aviation Training Weston Airways
G-AIFE	Proctor 2	E. G. Davis
G-AIFV	Freighter 21	Bristol Aeroplane Co.
G-AIFZ	Autocrat	L. Youngs
G-AIGC	Autocrat	Wiltshire School of Flying
G-AIGD	Autocrat	Loxhams Flying Services
G-AIGE	Autocrat	Southend Municipal Council
G-AIGF	Autocrat	F. J. R. Elliott
G-AIGG	Autocrat	H. Whitaker
G-AIGH	Autocrat	W. H. Binns
G-AIGI	Autocrat	Hunting Aerosurveys
G-AIGK	Autocrat	D. E. Harrington
G-AIGL	Autocrat	East Anglian Flying Services
G-AIGM	Autocrat	Eagle Aviation
G-AIGO	Autocrat	C. W. Blankley
G-AIGP	Autocrat	G. C. Wright
G-AIGR	Autocrat	Wolverhampton Aviation
G-AIGS	Autocrat	W. H. Byars
G-AIGT	Autocrat	H. N. R. Dale
G-AIGU	Autocrat	H. Mitchell
G-AIGV	Autocrat	G. C. Wright
G-AIGX	Autocrat	T. C. Fooks
G-AIGY	Autocrat	J. H. Watts & Ptns.
G-AIGZ	Auster J/4	H. F. Fulford
G-AIHB	Proctor 2	W. Vinter
G-AIHD	Proctor 3	Lancashire Aircraft Corp.
G-AIHE	Proctor 1	J. C. Hyland
G-AIHF	Proctor 1	Lancashire Aircraft Corp.
G-AIHG	Proctor 1	Air Enterprises
G-AIHH	Proctor 1	Lancashire Aircraft Corp.

Registration	Type	Owner or Operator
G-AIHK	Aerovan 3	S. G. Newport
G-AIHM	Gemini 1A	Ulster Aviation
G-AIHN	Dragon Rapide	Gibraltar Airways
G-AIHO	Tiger Moth	Coventry Aeroplane Club
G-AIHV	Halifax 8	Lancashire Aircraft Corp.
G-AIHX	Halifax 8	Lancashire Aircraft Corp.
G-AIIF	Gemini 1A	Cambridge University Flying Club
G-AIIG	Aerovan 3	Bowmaker Ltd.
G-AIIH	J–3C Cub	A. C. Cox
G-AIII	Proctor 1	Darlington & Dist. Aero Club
G-AIIK	Proctor 1	Field Aircraft Services
G-AIIL	Proctor 3	Olley Air Service
G-AIIP	Proctor 2	A. T. Leaning
G-AIIR	Proctor 1	Southend-on-Sea Flying Services
G-AIIS	Consul	International Airways
G-AIIT	Vega Gull	St. Christopher Travelways
G-AIIU	Taylorcraft D	Airways Aero Assoc.
G-AIIW	Proctor 1	Reid & Sigrist
G-AIIZ	Tiger Moth	L. T. (Central Buses) Sports Assoc.
G-AIJA	Tiger Moth	L.T. (Central Buses) Sports Assoc.
G-AIJD	Dakota 3	S. Rubin
G-AIJE	Viking 1	M.o.S. (B.E.A.C.)
G-AIJG	Autocrat	Cardiff Aeroplane Club
G-AIJH	Autocrat	R. E. Clive
G-AIJI	Autocrat	Britavia
G-AIJK	Auster J/4	Warwickshire Aero Club
G-AIJL	Auster J/4	R. H. Braime
G-AIJM	Auster J/4	P. Parry
G-AIJN	Auster J/4	H. Gadsby
G-AIJO	Auster J/4	Miss G. Pendleton
G-AIJP	Auster J/4	Skyfreight
G-AIJR	Auster J/4	Loxhams Flying Services
G-AIJS	Auster J/4	Auster Aircraft
G-AIJT	Auster J/4	Spa & Warwick Timber Co.
G-AIJW	Autocrat	Ten-Sixty-Six Products
G-AIJZ	Autocrat	Leek Hill Aviation (Birmingham)
G-AIKA	Auster 5	T. Shipside Ltd.
G-AIKC	Auster 5	J. H. Reyner
G-AIKE	Auster 5	J. Moore
G-AIKG	Proctor 1	C. G. Blanter
G-AIKI	Proctor 1	Brooklands Aviation
G-AIKJ	Proctor 3	Brooklands Aviation
G-AIKK	Proctor 1	Reid & Sigrist
G-AIKO	Consul	Chartair
G-AIKR	Consul	Airwork
G-AIKS	Consul	Bowmaker Ltd.
G-AIKT	Consul	Wirral Airways
G-AIKU	Consul	Butlins Ltd.
G-AIKX	Consul	Samuel Hodge & Sons
G-AIKZ	Consul	Bowmaker Ltd.
G-AILF	Aerovan 4	Western Manufacturing Estate
G-AILG	Gemini 1A	Neptune Continental Merchants
G-AILH	Marathon 1	M.o.S.
G-AILI	Messenger 2A	W. G. Breen-Turner
G-AILL	Messenger 2A	Air Schools Ltd.
G-AILM	Aerovan 4	Western Manufacturing Estate
G-AILN	Proctor 1	Field Aircraft Services

Registration	Type	Owner or Operator
G–AILO	Halifax 8	Lancashire Aircraft Corp.
G–AILP	Proctor I	Miss R. Rees
G–AILS	Tiger Moth	Herts & Essex Aero Club
G–AILT	Tiger Moth	Herts & Essex Aero Club
G–AIME	Freighter 21E	Bristol Aeroplane Co.
G–AIML	Brabazon 2	M.o.S.
G–AINY	Tiger Moth	Southend Municipal Council
G–AINZ	Anson I	Straight Aviation Training Weston Airways
G–AIOA	Anson I	Straight Aviation Training Weston Airways
G–AIOB	Anson I	Straight Aviation Training Weston Airways
G–AIOC	Cierva C.30A	G. S. Baker
G–AIOK	Hawk Trainer 3	Derby Aero Club
G–AIOP	Consul	Transair
G–AIOS	Consul	Morton Air Services
G–AIOT	Consul	Air Enterprises
G–AIOV	Consul	Air Enterprises
G–AIOW	Consul	Morton Air Services
G–AIOX	Consul	Flyaway
G–AIOY	Consul	Solar Air Services
G–AIPA	Anson I	College of Aeronautics
G–AIPB	Anson I	College of Aeronautics
G–AIPC	Anson I	College of Aeronautics
G–AIPD	Anson I	College of Aeronautics
G–AIPE	Auster 5	C. L. Bendall
G–AIPF	Auster 5	N. B. Williams & J. B. Hall
G–AIPG	Auster J/4	B. F. Francis
G–AIPH	Auster J/4	Wright Aviation
G–AIPI	Auster J/4	T. Shipside Ltd.
G–AIPJ	Auster J/4	T. Shipside Ltd.
G–AIPK	Auster J/4	Warwickshire Aero Club
G–AIPL	Auster J/4	Inter-City Airways
G–AIPM	Auster J/4	C. W. Blankley
G–AIPN	Auster 5	N. D. Roughsedge
G–AIPO	Auster 5	Fred Mellor (Wolverhampton)
G–AIPR	Auster J/4	H. C. N. Goodhart
G–AIPS	Auster J/4	Miss E. I. Kidner
G–AIPU	Autocrat	Aerial Spraying Contractors
G–AIPV	Autocrat	J. C. Wilson
G–AIPW	Autocrat	Miss R. H. Reeves
G–AIPY	Autocrat	Mrs. F. G. Myland
G–AIPZ	Autocrat	C. V. Young
G–AIRA	Autocrat	P. W. Scotney
G–AIRB	Autocrat	Inter-City Airways
G–AIRC	Autocrat	W. S. Shackleton
G–AIRD	Auster J/4	Boston Air Transport
G–AIRE	Taylorcraft D	R. J. Bowers
G–AIRI	Tiger Moth	West London Aero Club
G–AIRJ	Tiger Moth	West London Aero Club
G–AIRK	Tiger Moth	West London Aero Club
G–AIRM	Anson I	Aero & Engineering (Merseyside)
G–AIRN	Anson I	Aero & Engineering (Merseyside)
G–AIRP	Consul	Brevet Flying Club
G–AIRR	Tiger Moth	Short Bros. & Harland
G–AIRS	Gemini IA	M.C.A.
G–AIRW	Anson I	Airwork

Registration	Type	Owner or Operator
G–AIRX	Anson I	North Sea Air Transport
G–AIRY	Messenger 4	British Aviation Insurance Co.
G–AIRZ	Oxford I	B.O.A.C.
G–AISA	Tipsy B	R.N. Flying Club
G–AISB	Tipsy B	R.N. Flying Club
G–AISC	Tipsy B	Fairey Aviation Co.
G–AISE	Aerovan 4	British Nederland Airservices
G–AISF	Aerovan 4	T. C. Pick
G–AISI	Aerovan 4	Aviation Traders
G–AISK	Gemini IA	Sir Clifford Paterson
G–AISL	Messenger 2A	C. H. Simpson
G–AISM	Gemini IA	A. W. Sawyer
G–AISN	Gemini IA	J. Brockhouse & Co.
G–AISP	J–3C Cub	G. Reid-Walker
G–AISR	Tiger Moth	Hampshire School of Flying
G–AISU	Spitfire 5B	A. H. Wheeler
G–AISX	J–3C Cub	F. Smith
G–AITB	Oxford I	Air Service Training
G–AITD	Tiger Moth	Lockwoods Flying Services
G–AITE	Tiger Moth	D. Heaton
G–AITF	Oxford I	Air Service Training
G–AITI	Tiger Moth	Airwork Flying Club
G–AITJ	Anson I	Whitney Straight Ltd.
G–AITL	Anson I	Barclays International Airways
G–AITN	Hawk Trainer 3	Woodward & Son (Derby)
G–AITO	Hawk Trainer 3	East Riding Flying Club
G–AITS	Hawk Trainer 3	T. F. W. Gunton
G–AITZ	Hawk Trainer 3	H. V. Behar
G–AIUA	Hawk Trainer 3	R. H. Young
G–AIUB	Hawk Trainer 3	Universal Flying Services
G–AIUE	Hawk Trainer 3	T. C. Sparrow
G–AIUG	Hawk Trainer 3	R. G. Forbes-Bassett
G–AIUH	Oxford I	Reid & Sigrist
G–AIUK	Dragon Rapide	Air Schools
G–AIUL	Dragon Rapide	Air Transport (Charter) (C.I.)
G–AIUM	Dragon Rapide	Hunting Flying Clubs
G–AIUN	Dragon Rapide	Mayfair Air Services
G–AIUO	Dragon Rapide	Hornton Airways
G–AIUU	Consul	Thomas Barclay Ltd.
G–AIUW	Consul	Transair
G–AIUX	Consul	B.O.A.C. *Star Master*
G–AIUY	Consul	Olley Air Service
G–AIVA	Consul	Transair
G–AIVB	Viking IB	B.E.A.C. *Vernal*
G–AIVC	Viking IB	B.E.A.C. *Vernon*
G–AIVD	Viking IB	B.E.A.C. *Veteran*
G–AIVF	Viking IB	B.E.A.C. *Vibrant*
G–AIVG	Viking IB	B.E.A.C. *Viceroy*
G–AIVH	Viking IB	B.E.A.C. *Vicinity*
G–AIVI	Viking IB	B.E.A.C. *Victor*
G–AIVJ	Viking IB	B.E.A.C. *Victoria*
G–AIVK	Viking IB	B.E.A.C. *Victory*
G–AIVL	Viking IB	B.E.A.C. *Vigilant*
G–AIVM	Viking IB	B.E.A.C. *Vigorous*
G–AIVN	Viking IB	B.E.A.C. *Violent*
G–AIVO	Viking IB	B.E.A.C. *Villain*
G–AIVV	Tiger Moth	Newcastle Aero Club
G–AIVW	Tiger Moth	Newcastle Aero Club

Registration	Type	Owner or Operator
G-AIVX	Sealand 1	Short Bros. & Harland
G-AIVY	Oxford 1	B.O.A.C. *Star Mentor*
G-AIVZ	Tiger Moth	T. Shipside Ltd.
G-AIWA	Proctor 1	W. J. Twitchell
G-AIWC	Dakota 3	Skyways *Sky Dispatch*
G-AIWD	Dakota 3	Skyways *Sky Warrior*
G-AIWE	Dakota 3	Skyways *Sky Lancer*
G-AIWF	Dove 2	Silver City Airways
G-AIWN	Halifax 8	Payloads
G-AIWS	Gemini 1A	Mayfair Air Service
G-AIWT	Halifax 8	Payloads
G-AIWU	Walrus 2	Sir C. A. C. Hampson
G-AIWV	Anson 1	British Air Transport
G-AIWX	Anson 1	British Air Transport
G-AIXA	Taylorcraft D	Cotswold Aero Club
G-AIXB	Taylorcraft D	Denham Flying Club
G-AIXC	Argus 1	F. Bosworth
G-AIXD	Tiger Moth	D. Lloyd
G-AIXG	Tiger Moth	College of Aeronautics
G-AIXI	Tiger Moth	College of Aeronautics
G-AIXJ	Tiger Moth	College of Aeronautics
G-AIXL	Tiger Moth	Universal Flying Services
G-AIXM	Argus 2	J. J. Mackersey
G-AIXN	M–1C Sokol	G. Shaw
G-AIXO	Anson 1	Culliford Air Lines
G-AIXR	Viking 1B	Airwork
G-AIXS	Viking 1B	Airwork
G-AIXU	Anson 1	Gulf Aviation
G-AIXV	Anson 1	Tangiers Transport (London
G-AIXZ	Anson 1	Dennis Aviation
G-AIYA	Tudor Freighter 3	M.C.A.
G-AIYB	Hawk Trainer 3	Redhill Flying Club
G-AIYC	Hawk Trainer 3	Redhill Flying Club
G-AIYD	Hawk Trainer 3	Redhill Flying Club
G-AIYE	Dragon Rapide	Olley Air Services
G-AIYH	Proctor 1	Hunting Flying Clubs
G-AIYK	Avro 19/2	Hunting Air Travel
G-AIYL	Hawk Trainer 3	J. Neasham
G-AIYM	Tutor	A. P. Fraser
G-AIYN	Apollo	M.o.S.
G-AIYO	Argus 1	Womens Junior Air Corps.
G-AIYP	Dragon Rapide	V. H. Bellamy
G-AIYR	Dragon Rapide	Reid & Sigrist
G-AIYS	Leopard Moth	H. F. Buckmaster
G-AIYU	J–3C Cub	Community Flying Club
G-AIYV	J–3C Cub	A. J. Walter
G-AIYX	J–3C Cub	Denham Air Services
G-AIYY	Dragon Rapide	Reid & Sigrist
G-AIZA	Proctor 3	D. Stansfield
G-AIZB	Proctor 5	East Hull Press
G-AIZC	Proctor 5	Flyaway
G-AIZE	Argus 1	B. R. Companini
G-AIZF	Tiger Moth	Midland Bank Flying Club
G-AIZI	Dragon Rapide	Reid & Sigrist
G-AIZK	Hawk Trainer 3	J. P. Gunner
G-AIZL	Hawk Trainer 3	J. V. Green
G-AIZU	Autocrat	R. A. Davies (Birmingham)
G-AIZV	Autocrat	Herts & Essex Aero Club

Registration	Type	Owner or Operator
G-AIZW	Autocrat	Wiltshire School of Flying
G-AIZY	Autocrat	Hastings & East Sussex Air Service
G-AIZZ	Autocrat	Air Kruise (Kent)
G-AJAB	Autocrat	R. P. Sayer
G-AJAC	Autocrat	R. L. Hutchins
G-AJAE	Autocrat	Royal Artillery Aero Club
G-AJAG	Autocrat	Inter-City Air Services
G-AJAH	Autocrat	G. Hadman
G-AJAI	Autocrat	Fen Drains & Excavations
G-AJAJ	Autocrat	McVitie Price
G-AJAK	Auster 5	Eagle Aerophotos
G-AJAM	Arrow	B. Hynes
G-AJAN	Auster 5	E. P. Jenks Ltd.
G-AJAR	Autocrat	R. A. Pateman
G-AJAS	Autocrat	Hunting Flying Clubs
G-AJAT	Argus I	J. J. Hofer
G-AJAV	Dakota 3	Silver City Airways
G-AJAW	Lodestar	Silver City Airways
G-AJBF	Argus I	J. R. Grice (Thorne Aviation)
G-AJBH	Dakota 3	Lamberts Trust
G-AJBI	Dove I	Morton Air Services
G-AJBJ	Dragon Rapide	Birkett Air Service
G-AJBM	Viking IB	B.E.A.C. *Vincent*
G-AJBN	Viking IB	B.E.A.C. *Vindictive*
G-AJBO	Viking IB	B.E.A.C. *Vintage*
G-AJBP	Viking IB	B.E.A.C. *Vintner*
G-AJBR	Viking IB	B.E.A.C. *Virginia*
G-AJBS	Viking IB	B.E.A.C. *Virgo*
G-AJBT	Viking IB	B.E.A.C. *Viper*
G-AJBU	Viking IB	B.E.A.C. *Virtue*
G-AJBV	Viking IB	B.E.A.C. *Viscount*
G-AJBW	Viking IB	B.E.A.C. *Vista*
G-AJBX	Viking IB	B.E.A.C. *Vital*
G-AJBY	Viking IB	B.E.A.C. *Vitality*
G-AJCA	Viking IB	B.E.A.C. *Vixen*
G-AJCD	Viking IB	B.E.A.C. *Vizor*
G-AJCE	Viking IB	B.E.A.C. *Vivacious*
G-AJCK	Heath Parasol	Airways Aero Association
G-AJCL	Dragon Rapide	Allgood Manufacturing Co.
G-AJCM	Hawk Trainer 3	
G-AJCN	Proctor 3	A. Andrew
G-AJCO	Anson I	
G-AJCP	Anson I	
G-AJCR	Anson I	
G-AJCS	Anson I	
G-AJCT	Anson I	
G-AJCU	Proctor 3	F. J. R. Elliott
G-AJCV	Proctor 3	
G-AJCW	Proctor 3	
G-AJCX	Proctor 3	L. C. Hazard
G-AJCY	Proctor 3	M. Dumont
G-AJCZ	Proctor 3	J. R. Brittain
G-AJDA	Proctor 3	
G-AJDB	Proctor 3	
G-AJDC	Argus	
G-AJDF	Messenger 4A	N. B. Williams
G-AJDH	Avro 19	Secretary of State for Air
G-AJDI	Viking IB	B.E.A.C. *Volatile*

Registration	Type	Owner or Operator
G-AJDJ	Viking 1B	B.E.A.C. *Volley*
G-AJDK	Viking 1B	B.E.A.C. *Volunteer*
G-AJDL	Viking 1B	B.E.A.C. *Vortex*
G-AJDM	Messenger 2A	Boston Air Transport
G-AJDN	Dragon Rapide	Birkett Air Service
G-AJDO	Argus 1	H. Molt-Bignell
G-AJDP	Dove 1	Hunting Air Travel
G-AJDR	Hawk Trainer 3	
G-AJDS	J-3C Cub	A. J. Walter
G-AJDT	Argus	R. B. Pursey
G-AJDV	Autocrat	Universal Flying Services
G-AJDW	Autocrat	Brooklands Aviation
G-AJDY	Autocrat	P. J. S. Dredge
G-AJDZ	Autocrat	A. F. Johnson
G-AJEA	Autocrat	F. J. R. Elliott
G-AJEB	Autocrat	Hunting Aerosurveys
G-AJEC	Autocrat	Fen Drains & Excavations
G-AJED	Autocrat	Redhill Flying Club
G-AJEE	Autocrat	W. S. Shackleton
G-AJEF	Autocrat	British Air Transport
G-AJEH	Autocrat	Redhill Flying Club
G-AJEK	Autocrat	J. N. Williamson
G-AJEN	Autocrat	Loxhams Flying Service
G-AJEO	Autocrat	Southend Municipal Council
G-AJEP	Autocrat	Airwork
G-AJEU	Autocrat	G. A. Whittaker
G-AJEW	Autocrat	A. W. Bingham
G-AJEX	Gemini 1A	Modern Houses (Jersey)
G-AJEY	Messenger 2A	Thomas Carlyle
G-AJFC	Messenger 2A	T. Shipside Ltd.
G-AJFD	Gemini 1A	Bees Flight Ltd.
G-AJFE	Mercury 4C	J. F. Schumaker
G-AJFF	Messenger 2A	G. Clifton
G-AJFH	Messenger 2A	Ulster Aviation
G-AJFJ	Dragon Rapide	C. W. J. Allen
G-AJFK	Dragon Rapide	Island Air Charters
G-AJFR	Viking 1B	Airwork
G-AJFS	Viking 1B	Airwork
G-AJFT	Viking 1B	Airwork
G-AJFU	Sea Otter	British Aviation Services
G-AJFW	Sea Otter	British Aviation Services
G-AJFX	Anson 1	Blue Line Airways
G-AJGA	Consul	Lancashire Aircraft Corp.
G-AJGB	Consul	Barclays International Airways
G-AJGG	Consul	Chartair
G-AJGH	Consul	Air Charter
G-AJGJ	Auster 5	Walker & Thomson
G-AJGM	Hawk Trainer 3	Airways Aero Assoc.
G-AJGO	Proctor 1	Southern Aircraft (Gatwick)
G-AJGP	Hawk Trainer 3	M. W. R. Philp
G-AJGR	Oxford 1	Hunting Aerosurveys
G-AJGS	Dragon Rapide	Miss C. Brunning
G-AJGT	Dove 2	Airlinks
G-AJGU	Bristol 171	Bristol Aeroplane Co.
G-AJGV	Dragon Rapide	Manx Air Charter
G-AJGW	Argus 1	Aviation Traders
G-AJGY	Super Cruiser	C. G. Reid-Walker
G-AJHA	Hawk Trainer 3	E. D. Harris
G-AJHB	Hawk Trainer 3	Darlington & District Aero Club
G-AJHC	Hawk Trainer 3	J. Neasham

Registration	Type	Owner or Operator
G–AJHD	Hawk Trainer 3	J. Neasham
G–AJHG	Hawk Trainer 3	David C. Black & Co.
G–AJHI	Tiger Moth	Edinburgh Flying Club
G–AJHJ	Auster 5	Bertram Arden & Co.
G–AJHM	K.Z. Lark	Guernsey Salvage Co.
G–AJHO	Dragon Rapide	Brooklands Aviation
G–AJHP	Dragon Rapide	Brooklands Aviation
G–AJHR	Tiger Moth	Scottish Aviation
G–AJHS	Tiger Moth	Reid & Sigrist
G–AJHT	Tiger Moth	Reid & Sigrist
G–AJHU	Tiger Moth	Reid & Sigrist
G–AJHW	Sikorsky S–51	B.E.A.C.
G–AJHX	Dove I	Anglo-Iranian Oil Co.
G–AJHY	Dakota 3	B.E.A.C.
G–AJHZ	Dakota 3	B.E.A.C.
G–AJIA	Dakota 3	B.E.A.C.
G–AJIB	Dakota 3	B.E.A.C.
G–AJIC	Dakota 3	B.E.A.C.
G–AJID	Autocrat	A. C. Kingham
G–AJIE	Autocrat	A. L. Williams
G–AJIG	Autocrat	East Riding Flying Club
G–AJIH	Autocrat	Light Planes (Lancs)
G–AJII	Auster 5	F. C. Griffiths
G–AJIK	Auster 5	S. G. Newport
G–AJIN	Autocrat	East Riding Flying Club
G–AJIO	Autocrat	G. W. Barker
G–AJIP	Autocrat	Edinburgh Flying Club
G–AJIR	Autocrat	Mrs. D. B. Walker
G–AJIS	Autocrat	Russel Gunton
G–AJIT	Autocrat	Weston Aero Club
G–AJIU	Autocrat	G. Clifton & C. H. Wellband
G–AJIV	Autocrat	G. N. Drake
G–AJIW	Autocrat	W. H. & J. Rogers (Engineers)
G–AJIX	Autocrat	A. & Mrs. J. A. Bailey
G–AJIY	Autocrat	J. R. Ratcliffe
G–AJIZ	Autocrat J.I.A.	Auster Aircraft
G–AJJB	Auster 5	Bristol & Wessex Aero Club
G–AJJE	Beech D–17–S	David Brown and Sons (Huddersfield)
G–AJJF	Dove I	Iraq Petroleum Transport Co.
G–AJJG	Auster 5	T. W. Hayhow
G–AJJH	Auster 5A	F. M. J. H. de Malet-Rocquefort
G–AJJI	Hawk Trainer 3	R. N. H. Courtney
G–AJJJ	Beech 17	A. R. Pilgrim
G–AJJN	Viking IB	B.E.A.C. Vulcan
G–AJJP	Gyrodyne	Fairey Aviation Co.
G–AJJR	Auster 5	O. Hill & F. E. A. Mitchell
G–AJKC	Tudor Freighter 3	M.C.A.
G–AJKD	Tiger Moth	Midland Aero Club
G–AJKE	Dragon Rapide	W. A. Rollason Ltd.
G–AJKG	Messenger 2A	N. B. Williams
G–AJKH	Dragon Rapide	Anglo-Iranian Oil Co.
G–AJKI	Dragon Rapide	Anglo-Iranian Oil Co.
G–AJKK	Messenger 2A	Westfield Transport
G–AJKL	Messenger 2A	J. Fusco
G–AJKP	Aerovan 4	Patrick Motors
G–AJKR	Gemini IA	W. Stevens
G–AJKS	Gemini IA	British Aviation Insurance
G–AJKT	Messenger 2A	G. O. Lawford

Registration	Type	Owner or Operator
G–AJKU	Aerovan 4	Ulster Aviation
G–AJKV	Gemini 1A	A. Ercolani
G–AJKW	Dragon Rapide	Lancashire Aircraft Corp.
G–AJKX	Dragon Rapide	Lancashire Aircraft Corp.
G–AJKY	Dragon Rapide	Lancashire Aircraft Corp.
G–AJLE	Auster 5	Lancashire Aircraft Corp.
G–AJLG	Auster 4	Lancashire Aircraft Corp.
G–AJLH	Consul	Lancashire Aircraft Corp.
G–AJLI	Consul	Fairflight
G–AJLK	Consul	J. Patient
G–AJLM	Consul	J. T. Donaldson
G–AJLN	Consul	English Electric Co.
G–AJLP	Consul	Flyaway Ltd.
G–AJLR	Consul	Olley Air Services
G–AJLS	Proctor 1	D. C. T. Bennett
G–AJLT	Sea Otter	B.O.A.C.
G–AJLU	Sea Otter	B.O.A.C.
G–AJLV	Dove 1	M.C.A.
G–AJLW	Dove 2	De Havilland Aircraft Co.
G–AJLX	Dakota 3	Scottish Aviation
G–AJMA	Dove 1	M.C.A.
G–AJMH	Proctor 4	E. Williams
G–AJMI	Proctor 4	Whitehouse Industries
G–AJMK	Proctor 4	Field Aircraft Services
G–AJMP	Proctor 4	G. C. S. Whyman
G–AJMV	Proctor 4	British Syphon Co.
G–AJMW	Proctor 4	Short Bros. & Harland
G–AJMX	Proctor 4	Short Bros. & Harland
G–AJMY	Dragon Rapide	Sivewright Airways
G–AJMZ	Sandringham 5	B.O.A.C. *Perth*
G–AJNC	Oxford	Fairey Aviation Co.
G–AJNE	Consul	Air Enterprises
G–AJNG	Consul	Chartair
G–AJNN	Argus 1	F. A. Laker
G–AJNO	Walrus 1	Scottish Aviation
G–AJNP	Walrus 1	Scottish Aviation
G–AJNT	Halifax 8	Payloads
G–AJNV	Halifax 8	Payloads
G–AJNW	Halifax 8	Westminster Airways
G–AJOA	Tiger Moth	Short Bros. & Harland
G–AJOB	Aerovan 4	Ulster Aviation
G–AJOC	Messenger 2A	C. E. Hickman
G–AJOD	Messenger 2A	Claremont Shipping Co.
G–AJOE	Messenger 2A	Reproducers & Amplifiers
G–AJOF	Aerovan 4	Patrick Motors
G–AJOG	Aerovan 4	North Sea Air Transport
G–AJOH	Gemini 1A	J. R. A. Stroyan
G–AJOI	Aerovan 4	Sivewright Airways
G–AJOJ	Gemini 1A	Loxhams Flying Services
G–AJOK	Gemini 1A	Fairey Aviation Co.
G–AJOM	Gemini 1A	Sir Alexander Gibb
G–AJOO	Sikorsky S–51	Pest Control
G–AJOP	Sikorsky S–51	
G–AJOR	Sikorsky S–51	B.E.A.C.
G–AJOT	Dove 1	Olley Air Services
G–AJOV	Sikorsky S–51	B.E.A.C.
G–AJOW	Argus	P. MacKisray
G–AJOX	Argus 1	J. G. Crampton

Registration	Type	Owner or Operator
G–AJOZ	Argus I	Weston Aero Club
G–AJPA	Argus I	Weston Aero Club
G–AJPC	Argus I	G. Clifton
G–AJPD	Argus I	Weston Aero Club
G–AJPE	Argus	Aviation Traders
G–AJPF	Dakota 3	Trent Valley Aviation
G–AJPH	Viking (Nene)	M.o.S.
G–AJPI	Argus I	West London Aero Club
G–AJPR	Dove I	B.O.A.C.
G–AJPS	Arrow	Somerton Airways
G–AJPU	Arrow	J. M. Rollo
G–AJPW	Autocrat	Duncan Smith & Co.
G–AJPX	Autocrat	W. Midlands Erection Co.
G–AJPY	Autocrat	T. Shipside Ltd.
G–AJRB	Autocrat	Brooklands Aviation
G–AJRC	Autocrat	Lancashire Aircraft Corp.
G–AJRE	Autocrat	W. Hutchinson
G–AJRF	Autocrat	Aero Industries
G–AJRG	Autocrat	Mrs. E. F. Slade
G–AJRH	Autocrat	Auster Aircraft
G–AJRK	Autocrat	N. West
G–AJRN	Autocrat	Auster Aircraft
G–AJRO	Autocrat	Auster Aircraft
G–AJRP	Autocrat	H. A. Sissons
G–AJRR	Arrow	Auster Aircraft
G–AJRS	Hawk Trainer 3	British Air Transport
G–AJRT	Hawk Trainer 3	British Air Transport
G–AJRU	Hawk Trainer 3	British Air Transport
G–AJRV	Hawk Trainer 3	Darlington & District Aero Club
G–AJRZ	Argus I	West London Aero Club
G–AJSE	Anson I	E. E. McIlree
G–AJSF	Hawk Trainer 3	W. Holderness
G–AJSG	Argus I	L. D. Hawthorn
G–AJSH	Argus I	L. D. Hawthorn
G–AJSK	Dragon Rapide	B.E.A.C.
G–AJSL	Dragon Rapide	Trent Valley Aviation
G–AJSN	Argus I	Hon. B. L. Bathurst
G–AJSO	Argus I	West London Aero Club
G–AJSP	Argus I	J. J. Hofer
G–AJSR	Argus I	Pasolds
G–AJSS	Argus I	Suffolk Trust
G–AJSZ	Halifax 8	Lancashire Aircraft Corp.
G–AJTB	Gemini 1A	C. F. L. Hersee
G–AJTC	Aerovan 4	Western Manufacturing Estate
G–AJTG	Gemini 1B	Hon. Max Aitken
G–AJTK	Aerovan 4	British Nederland Airservices
G–AJTL	Gemini 1A	A.B.C. Motor Co.
G–AJTM	Auster 5	Wiltshire School of Flying
G–AJTN	Auster 5	Wiltshire School of Flying
G–AJTO	Dakota 3	Zinc Corporation
G–AJTP	Proctor 4	Newman Aircraft
G–AJTR	Argus I	Taylor Electrical Instruments
G–AJTV	Auster 5	G. Bukley
G–AJTW	Tiger Moth	Short Bros. & Harland
G–AJUC	Autocrat	
G–AJUD	Autocrat	Auster Aircraft
G–AJUE	Autocrat	Darlington & District Aero Club
G–AJUF	Autocrat	Auster Aircraft

Registration	Type	Owner or Operator
G-AJUH	Autocrat	C. H. Webb
G-AJUJ	Autocrat	Weston Aero Club
G-AJUK	Autocrat	Southend Municipal Council
G-AJUL	Autocrat	Loxhams Flying Services
G-AJUM	Autocrat	Weston Aero Club
G-AJUN	Autocrat	W. Petrie-Hay
G-AJUO	Autocrat	Weston Aero Club
G-AJUP	Autocrat	Southend Municipal Council
G-AJUR	Autocrat	J. E. Coxon
G-AJUW	Aiglet J/1B	Ariel Spraying Contractors
G-AJUY	Autocrat	Auster Aircraft
G-AJUZ	Autocrat	Miss M. Kelly
G-AJVA	Dragon Rapide	Iraq Petroleum Transport Co.
G-AJVB	Dragon Rapide	Iraq Petroleum Transport Co.
G-AJVC	Messenger 2A	Lionel Sage & Co.
G-AJVD	Chipmunk	de Havilland Aircraft Co.
G-AJVE	Tiger Moth	
G-AJVF	Tiger Moth	McDonald Aircraft
G-AJVI	Argus I	S. K. Davies
G-AJVM	Argus	West London Aero Club
G-AJVN	Auster 5	J. J. Mackersey
G-AJVT	Auster 5	Anglo-Continental Air Services
G-AJVU	Auster 5	L. W. Watkins
G-AJVV	Auster 5	Birmingham Aero Club
G-AJVY	Dakota 3	London Express Newspapers
G-AJVZ	Dakota 3	Lambert Bros.
G-AJWA	Gemini IA	J. J. Hofer
G-AJWB	Messenger 2A	Wiltshire School of Flying
G-AJWC	Gemini IA	Derek Crouch (Contractors)
G-AJWD	Aerovan 4	Western Manufacturing Estate
G-AJWE	Gemini IA	Scaffolding (G.B.)
G-AJWF	Gemini IA	Guernsey Salvage Co.
G-AJWG	Gemini IA	J. W. Adamson
G-AJWH	Gemini IA	R. J. B. Pearse
G-AJWI	Aerovan 4	Mayfair Air Services
G-AJWL	Gemini IA	Air Charter
G-AJXA	Argus I	D. B. Munro
G-AJXB	Dragon Rapide	B.E.A.C.
G-AJXC	Auster 5	A. H. Warminger
G-AJXE	Consul	M.C.A.
G-AJXF	Consul	M.C.A.
G-AJXG	Consul	M.C.A.
G-AJXH	Consul	M.C.A.
G-AJXI	Consul	M.C.A.
G-AJXO	Autocrat	R. K. Dundas
G-AJXS	Autocrat	Westland Aircraft
G-AJXX	Auster 5	T. W. Hayhow
G-AJXY	Auster 5	T. W. Leadbetter
G-AJXZ	Arrow	A. S. Mackenzie-Lowe
G-AJYB	Auster 5	J. G. Crampton
G-AJYD	Auster 5	Le Bryan Group Products
G-AJYG	Auster J/5	Auster Aircraft
G-AJYI	Auster 5	F. L. de Rosnay
G-AJYK	Autocar	Airviews
G-AJYL	Auster J/5	Auster Aircraft
G-AJYN	Autocar	J. V. Henz-Smith
G-AJYP	Auster 4	R. Pointer
G-AJYS	Avis 2	Auster Aircraft

Top : Short SOLENT. Largest of the supremely comfortable and reliable Short flying boats used by B.O.A.C., the Solents were used on the *Springbok* route to South Africa.

Centre : Handley Page HERMES V. This version of the Hermes, powered by four Theseus "propjets," is basically similar to the Hercules-engined Mark IV, twenty-five of which will be operated by B.O.A.C.

Bottom : S.I.A.I. S.M.95. Largest Italian civil air liner in service, the 36-seat S.M.95 is operated into London Airport by Alitalia.
(*B.E.A. photo.*)

Left : Bristol FREIGHTER
Designed as a "utility"
cargo-carrying aircraft with-
out any frills, the Freighter
set a new fashion with its
large sideways-opening
nose doors and capacious
fuselage. G–AICM, shown
here in Iran, is used by
Hunting Aerosurveys for
aerial photography.

Below : Vickers VISCOUNT·
World's first "prop-jet"-
powered air liner, the
Viscount is in production for
B.E.A. It will bring Rome
within four hours of London,
by cruising at up to 300
m.p.h.

Below : S.E.161
LANGUEDOC.
Although design-
ed pre-war, the
Languedoc is
reliable and
comfortable
even by modern
standards. It is
used extensively
on Air France's
medium-range
services. *(F. G.
Swanborough.)*

Right : Iliushin IL-12 The IL-12, operated by Czech Airlines, is the only modern Russian aeroplane seen in this country since the war. (*F. G. Swanborough.*)

Left : de Havilland DOVE. More than 300 of these little 8-11 seat air liners are in service all over the world.

Right : CONVAIR-LINER. This 40-passenger "twin" is America's most popular post-war replacement for the veteran Dakota. (*K.L.M. photo.*)

Left : Vickers VIKING. Mainstay of B.E.A.'s fleet since the war. The Viking shown here is one of four belonging to the King's Flight.

Below:
RAPIDE.
popular lig
built, the
giving fine
routes an
'plane. (B

Above : Short SEALAND.
One of the most versatile
aircraft flying, the little
Sealand can be used as a
passenger air liner, freighter
or air ambulance, from land
or water bases. (*Flight photo.*)

Below : Avro XIX. Developed
from the R.A.F.'s Anson, and
sharing that aircraft's superb
tradition of safety and reli-
ability, the Avro XIX is
widely used by British
charter companies.

avilland
f the most
liners ever
le is still
e on short
a joy-ride
oto.)

Above : Percival PRINCE.
Designed as a light air liner
the Prince is used also as a
" flying class-room " by the
Royal Navy and, with modi-
fied nose, as shown here, for
air survey work.

Below : Vickers SEA OTTER.
This ex-R.A.F. air-sea rescue
Sea Otter is now being
flown in Venezuela by the
Royal Dutch Shell Company
and no longer appears on the
British register.

Left: Douglas DC–3. World's most famous air liner, the DC–3 Dakota is still in large-scale service in every continent. Altogether, more than 10,000 of these aircraft were built, mostly during the war, when they were standard transport equipment of the Allied airborne armies. (*K.L.M. photo.*)

Right : Handley Page MARATHON I. Soon to go into service on B.E.A.'s shorter routes. G–ALVW is one of the more recent aircraft on register.

Below : Airspeed AMBASSADOR. Twenty of these graceful 49-seat air liners are on order for B.E.A.

Right : Auster AUTO-CAR. Latest of the well-known Auster series of light 'planes, the Autocar is Britain's lowest-priced four-seater.

Below : Chrislea SUPER ACE. Tricycle undercarriage and twin fins and rudders characterize the Super Ace, many of which have been exported since the war. (*John W. R. Taylor.*)

Below : Miles MART-LET and GEMINI. First aircraft built by F. G. Miles, the biplane Martlet of 1929 is here seen in flight with a twin-engine Gemini, one of the last and most popular of the Miles civil types. A Gemini won the first post-war race for the King's Cup in 1949.

Above : *Auster* AUTOCRAT. Most widely-used British light 'plane. The aircraft shown here is specially equipped with public address loud speakers and castering wheels, which enable it to land safely cross-wind.

Left : *Fairey* PRIMER. Developed from a pre-war design of the Belgian Avions Fairey Company, the Primer has an unusual hood arrangement, giving an exceptional view from the rear cockpit.

Below : *Tipsy* TRAINER. Another Avions Fairey design the Tipsy side-by-side two-seat Trainer is used by the Royal Naval Flying Club and several British private owners.

Registration	Type	Owner or Operator
G–AJZD	Dakota 3	British Nederland Airservices
G–AJZG	Aerovan 4	Culliford Airlines
G–AJZH	Hawk Trainer 3	P. J. McNamara
G–AJZJ	Gemini 1A	Air Schools
G–AJZL	Gemini 1A	M.C.A.
G–AJZN	Aerovan 4	Air Schools
G–AJZO	Gemini 1A	Whitbread & Co.
G–AJZS	Gemini 1A	J. J. Hofer
G–AJZT	Dove 2	H.H. Prince Aly Khan
G–AJZW	Viscount	Vickers-Armstrongs Ltd.
G–AJZX	Dakota 3	British Nederland Airservices
G–AJZY	Halifax 8	Lancashire Aircraft Corp.
G–AKAA	J–3C Cub	Airborne Taxi Services
G–AKAI	Messenger 2A	Harben Aviation
G–AKAJ	Lancaster 1	Flight Refuelling
G–AKAK	Lancaster 1	Flight Refuelling
G–AKAL	Lancaster 1	Flight Refuelling
G–AKAM	Lancaster 1	Flight Refuelling
G–AKAN	Messenger 2A	G. McLean
G–AKAO	Messenger 2A	E. G. Lamb
G–AKAP	Halifax 6	
G–AKAR	Dakota 4	Kearsley Airways
G–AKAS	Hawk Trainer 3	Essex Aero
G–AKAT	Hawk Trainer 3	Essex Aero
G–AKAU	Hawk Trainer 3	Essex Aero
G–AKAV	Messenger 2A	W. H. Byars
G–AKAX	Bucker Bu 181	O. F. Maclaren
G–AKAY	Dakota 3	Sivewright Airways
G–AKBE	Concordia 1	Cunliffe-Owen Aircraft
G–AKBF	Prestwick Pioneer 2	Scottish Aviation
G–AKBG	Viking 1B	B.E.A.C. *Votary*
G–AKBH	Viking 1B	B.E.A.C. *Voyager*
G–AKBI	Halifax 3	Lancashire Aircraft Corp.
G–AKBK	Halifax 8	Lancashire Aircraft Corp.
G–AKBM	Messenger 2A	Plymouth & District Aero Club
G–AKBN	Messenger 2A	W. P. Bowles
G–AKBO	Messenger 2A	Air Schools
G–AKBR	Halifax 8	Eagle Aviation
G–AKBV	J–3C Cub	A. J. Walter
G–AKBZ	Tudor 5	B.O.A.C. *Star Falcon*
G–AKCA	Tudor 5	B.O.A.C. *Star Hawk*
G–AKCB	Tudor 5	B.O.A.C. *Star Kestrel*
G–AKCC	Tudor 5	William Dempster *President Kruger*
G–AKCD	Tudor 5	B.O.A.C. *Star Eagle*
G–AKCE	Constellation	B.O.A.C. *Bedford*
G–AKCF	Dove	B.O.A.C.
G–AKCG	Tiger Moth	Airwork
G–AKCH	Tiger Moth	Scottish Flying Club
G–AKCI	Tiger Moth	Scottish Flying Club
G–AKCJ	Argus 1	Air Navigation & Trading Co.
G–AKCM	Tiger Moth	Airwork
G–AKCN	Messenger 2A	T. Shipside Ltd.
G–AKCO	Sandringham 7	B.O.A.C. *St. George*
G–AKCP	Sandringham 7	B.O.A.C. *St. David*
G–AKCR	Sandringham 7	B.O.A.C. *St. Andrew*
G–AKCS	Chipmunk	Loxhams Flying Services
G–AKCZ	Beech C/18–S	Britavia
G–AKDA	Gemini 1A	Patrick Duval Aviation

Registration	Type	Owner or Operator
G-AKDB	Gemini 1A	McCowan & Cross
G-AKDC	Gemini 3	J. N. Somers
G-AKDD	Gemini 1A	M.C.A.
G-AKDE	Gemini 1A	L. Roper
G-AKDF	Messenger 2A	Longford Engineering Co.
G-AKDG	Gemini 1A	S. E. Norman
G-AKDH	Gemini 1A	Field Aircraft Services
G-AKDI	Gemini 1A	P. P. Bradley
G-AKDJ	Gemini 1A	Hornton Airways
G-AKDK	Gemini 1A	W/Cdr. H. C. Kennard
G-AKDL	Gemini 1A	N. R. L. Urquhart
G-AKDM	Super Cruiser	E. C. S. Harper
G-AKDN	Chipmunk	de Havilland Aircraft Co.
G-AKDO	Lancastrian 4	⎫
G-AKDR	Lancastrian 4	⎬ Flight Refuelling
G-AKDS	Lancastrian 4	⎭
G-AKDT	Dakota 4	Kearsley Airways
G-AKDU	Avro 19	Secretary of State for Colonies
G-AKDV	Avro 19	Secretary of State for Colonies
G-AKDW	Dragon Rapide	Short Bros. & Harland
G-AKDX	Dragon Rapide	World Evangelisation Trust
G-AKDZ	Proctor 5	W. Stevens
G-AKEA	Proctor 5	N. King
G-AKEB	Proctor 5	William Wilson & Son
G-AKEC	Halifax 8	Lancashire Aircraft Corp.
G-AKED	Dragon Rapide	W. M. Andrews
G-AKEF	Proctor 4	E. R. Pyatt
G-AKEG	Gemini 1A	S. G. Newport
G-AKEH	Gemini 1A	H. H. E. M. Winch
G-AKEI	Gemini 1A	North Sea Air Transport
G-AKEJ	Gemini 1A	Ulster Aviation
G-AKEK	Gemini 1A	M. H. P. McAlpine
G-AKEL	Gemini 1A	D. Macartney-Filgate
G-AKEM	Gemini 1A	N. Rodnight
G-AKEN	Gemini 1A	C. R. Mauritzen
G-AKEP	Gemini 1A	Mayfair Air Services
G-AKER	Gemini 1A	Wallis & Linnell
G-AKES	Gemini 1A	T. Carlyle
G-AKET	Dove 1	Mrs. P. Churchill
G-AKEU	Dragon Rapide	Iraq Petroleum Transport Co.
G-AKEV	Chipmunk	de Havilland Aircraft Co.
G-AKEX	Proctor 1	H. C. V. Hext
G-AKEY	Slingsby T.29A	Slingsby Sailplanes
G-AKEZ	Messenger 2A	M. & H. Mining Contractors
G-AKFA	Bell 47 B3	B.E.A.C.
G-AKFB	Bell 47 B3	B.E.A.C.
G-AKFE	Avro 19/2	Secretary of State for Air
G-AKFF	Lancastrian 4	Flight Refuelling
G-AKFG	Lancastrian 4	Flight Refuelling
G-AKFK	Anson 1	Olds Discount Co.
G-AKFM	Anson 1	Finglands Airways
G-AKFN	Argus 1	L. D. Hawthorn
G-AKFO	Dragon Rapide	Southern Aircraft (Gatwick)
G-AKFP	Hermes 4	B.O.A.C. Hamilcar
G-AKFR	Proctor 4	Lancashire Aircraft Corp.
G-AKFS	Proctor 4	Lancashire Aircraft Corp.
G-AKFT	Proctor 4	Lancashire Aircraft Corp.
G-AKFU	Gemini 1A	West Midlands Erection Co.

Registration	Type	Owner or Operator
G-AKFX	Gemini 1A	Western Manufacturing Estate
G-AKFY	Gemini 1A	H. V. Kennedy
G-AKGA	Gemini 1A	Air Charter
G-AKGC	Gemini 1A	T. Shipside Ltd.
G-AKGD	Gemini 1A	Sivewright Airways
G-AKGE	Gemini 1A	Goodyear Tyre & Rubber Co. (G B.)
G-AKGF	Tiger Moth	London Transport (Central Buses) Sports Assoc.
G-AKGG	Tiger Moth	W. A. Rollason
G-AKGH	Stratocruiser	B.O.A.C. *Caledonia*
G-AKGI	Stratocruiser	B.O.A.C. *Caribou*
G-AKGJ	Stratocruiser	B.O.A.C. *Cambria*
G-AKGK	Stratocruiser	B.O.A.C. *Canopus*
G-AKGL	Stratocruiser	B.O.A.C. *Cabot*
G-AKGM	Stratocruiser	B.O.A.C. *Caster*
G-AKGN	Halifax 8	Chartair Ltd.
G-AKGO	Halifax 8	Airtech
G-AKGR	Hawk Trainer 3	Bournemouth Flying Club
G-AKGS	Hawk Trainer 3	Bournemouth Flying Club
G-AKGV	Dragon Rapide	William Dempster
G-AKGW	Argus	E. J. Farrow
G-AKGX	Dakota 3	Cyprus Airways
G-AKGY	Dragon Rapide	Manx Air Charters
G-AKHB	Gemini 1A	R. E. Bibby
G-AKHC	Gemini 1A	K. A. Hogan
G-AKHE	Gemini 1A	W. Hutchinson
G-AKHF	Aerovan 6	Avia Britannia Corporation
G-AKHG	Aerovan 4	S. G. Newport
G-AKHJ	Gemini 1A	Field Aircraft Services
G-AKHK	Gemini 1A	Loxhams Flying Services
G-AKHP	Gemini 1A	C. S. Thomas
G-AKHS	Gemini 1A	Mrs. A. Leadbetter
G-AKHV	Gemini 1A	W. T. Franklin
G-AKHW	Gemini 1A	B.O.A.C.
G-AKHX	Gemini 1A	Brooklands Aviation
G-AKHY	Gemini 1A	Hon. M. A. R. Cayzer
G-AKHZ	Gemini 1A	Pasolds
G-AKIA	Walrus 2	Ciro's Aviation
G-AKIC	Sea Otter	Ciro s Aviation
G-AKID	Sea Otter	Ciro's Aviation
G-AKIF	Dragon Rapide	Manx Air Charters
G-AKIG	Tiger Moth	D. Goldstein
G-AKIH	Proctor 5	Hon. E. H. K. Digby
G-AKII	Dakota 3	Cyprus Airways
G-AKIJ	Dakota 3	Cyprus Airways
G-AKIK	Dakota 3	Cyprus Airways
G-AKIL	Dakota 3	Air Transport (Charter) (C.I.)
G-AKIM	Messenger 2A	C. Screen
G-AKIN	Messenger 2A	A. J. Spiller
G-AKIO	Messenger 2A	Bidgood & Catton Taxi Planes
G-AKIR	Messenger 2A	P. Blamire
G-AKIS	Messenger 2A	Porter Spiers (Leicester)
G-AKIU	Proctor 5	Rolls-Royce
G-AKIW	Proctor 5	N. S. Norway
G-AKIX	Proctor 5	Shell Co. of Egypt
G-AKIY	Tiger Moth	Scottish Flying Club
G-AKIZ	Argus 1	A. J. Walter
G-AKJA	Argus 1	R. L. Whyham

43

Registration	Type	Owner or Operator
G-AKJD	Martin Hearn TQX–I	
G-AKJE	Walrus	Ciro's Aviation
G-AKJG	Dove 2	Silver City Airways
G-AKJH	Dakota 3	H.H. the Maharaja of Baroda
G-AKJL	Argus I	R. G. Kellett
G-AKJM	Argus I	W. S. Shackleton
G-AKJN	Dakota 3	Ciro's Aviation
G-AKJP	Dove 2	Silver City Airways
G-AKJR	Dove 2	Olley Air Service
G-AKJS	Dragon Rapide	Fairey Aviation Co.
G-AKJT	Auster 5	Wiltshire School of Flying
G-AKJU	Auster 5	Wiltshire School of Flying
G-AKJV	Hawk Trainer 3	Short Bros. & Harland
G-AKJX	Hawk Trainer 3	H. C. Kennard
G-AKJY	Dragon Rapide	Brooklands Aviation
G-AKJZ	Dragon Rapide	East Anglian Flying Services
G-AKKB	Gemini IA	F. Dunkerley
G-AKKC	Messenger 2A	J. M. Wilkinson
G-AKKF	Gemini IA	D. Ross
G-AKKG	Messenger 4A	Shell Mex & B.P.
G-AKKH	Gemini IA	S. Bourne & Co.
G-AKKI	Messenger 2A	J. Patson
G-AKKJ	Aerovan 4	
G-AKKK	Messenger 2A	Boston Air Transport
G-AKKL	Messenger 2A	Godfrey Holmes Ltd.
G-AKKN	Messenger 2A	P. S. Murphey
G-AKKO	Messenger 2A	T. Shipside Ltd.
G-AKKP	Halifax 9	Aviation Traders
G-AKKR	Hawk Trainer 3	
G-AKKS	Hawk Trainer 3	Airways Aero Assoc.
G-AKKU	Halifax 9	Aviation Traders
G-AKKV	Hawk Trainer 3	Airways Aero Assoc.
G-AKKW	Hawk Trainer 3	Airways Aero Assoc.
G-AKKX	Hawk Trainer 3	Airways Aero Assoc.
G-AKKY	Hawk Trainer 3	Airways Aero Assoc.
G-AKKZ	Hawk Trainer 3	Airways Aero Assoc.
G-AKLA	Dragon Rapide	Lancashire Aircraft Corp.
G-AKLB	Proctor 4	Lancashire Aircraft Corp
G-AKLD	Proctor 4	Lancashire Aircraft Corp
G-AKLG	Prentice I	Percival Aircraft
G-AKLL	Dakota 3	Hornton Airways
G-AKLN	Sealand I	Short Bros. & Harland
G-AKLO	Sealand	Short Bros. & Harland
G-AKLR	Sealand	Short Bros. & Harland
G-AKLS	Sealand	Short Bros. & Harland
G-AKLT	Sealand	Short Bros. & Harland
G-AKLU	Sealand	Short Bros. & Harland
G-AKLV	Sealand	Short Bros. & Harland
G-AKLW	Sealand	Short Bros. & Harland
G-AKLX	Sealand	Short Bros. & Harland
G-AKLZ	Sealand	Short Bros. & Harland
G-AKMA	Sealand	Short Bros. & Harland
G-AKMB	Auster 5	W. Brazier
G-AKMC	Auster 5	W. S. Shackleton
G-AKMD	Dragon Rapide	Aviation Traders
G-AKME	Dragon Rapide	Tyne Taxis
G-AKMF	Dragon Rapide	Mayfair Air Services
G-AKMG	Dragon Rapide	Sivewright Airways

Registration	Type	Owner or Operator
G–AKMH	Dragon Rapide	I.o.W. Flying Club
G–AKMI	Auster 5	P. L. Chadwick
G–AKMJ	Hawk Trainer 3	J. E. Tomlinson
G–AKMN	Hawk Trainer 3	L. D. Trappitt
G–AKMR	Hawk Trainer 3	L. D. Trappitt
G–AKMU	Hawk Trainer 3	C. J. de Vere
G–AKMV	Anson I	Airwork
G–AKMW	Lancastrian 2	Skyways
G–AKMX	Tiger Moth	Herts & Essex Aero Club
G–AKMY	Hawk Trainer 3	Herts & Essex Aero Club
G–AKMZ	Hawk Trainer 3	Herts & Essex Aero Club
G–AKNA	Hawk Trainer 3	Herts & Essex Aero Club
G–AKNE	Dragon Rapide	M. L. Thomas
G–AKNF	Dragon Rapide	Airlines (Jersey)
G–AKNG	Halifax 6	Lancashire Aircraft Corp.
G–AKNH	Halifax 6	Lancashire Aircraft Corp.
G–AKNI	Halifax 6	Lancashire Aircraft Corp.
G–AKNK	Halifax 6	Lancashire Aircraft Corp.
G–AKNL	Halifax 6	Lancashire Aircraft Corp.
G–AKNM	Dakota 4	Scottish Aviation
G–AKNN	Dragon Rapide	Astral Aviation
G–AKNO	Solent 3	M.C.A. *City of London*
G–AKNP	Solent 3	M.C.A. *City of Cardiff*
G–AKNR	Solent 3	M.C.A. *City of Belfast*
G–AKNS	Solent 3	M.C.A. *City of Liverpool*
G–AKNT	Solent 3	M.C.A.
G–AKNU	Solent 3	M.C.A.
G–AKNV	Dragon Rapide	Lancashire Aircraft Corp.
G–AKNW	Dragon Rapide	R. L. Whyham
G–AKNX	Dragon Rapide	Patrick Motors
G–AKNY	Dragon Rapide	Patrick Motors
G–AKOA	Dragon Rapide	Patrick Motors
G–AKOB	Dragon Rapide	Air Enterprises
G–AKOD	Dragon Rapide	Lancashire Aircraft Corp.
G–AKOE	Dragon Rapide	Lancashire Aircraft Corp.
G–AKOF	Dragon Rapide	Mannin Airways
G–AKOG	Dragon Rapide	Aviation Traders
G–AKOH	Dragon Rapide	Mannin Airways
G–AKOK	Dragon Rapide	Mannin Airways
G–AKOL	Hawk Trainer 3	S. R. C. Partridge
G–AKOM	Dragon Rapide	Southern Aircraft (Gatwick)
G–AKOO	Dragon Rapide	Southern Aircraft (Gatwick)
G–AKOR	Dragon Rapide	Morton Air Services
G–AKOT	Auster 5	A. D. Daly
G–AKOU	Auster 5	C. F. Westley
G–AKOV	Dragon Rapide	Inter-City Air Services
G–AKOW	Auster 5	J. Small
G–AKOX	Auster 5	N. C. Anderson
G–AKOY	Dragon Rapide	Lancashire Aircraft Corp.
G–AKOZ	Dakota 4	Kearsley Airways
G–AKPA	Dragon Rapide	Newman Aircraft Co.
G–AKPE	Hawk Trainer 3	D. C. Jennett
G–AKPF	Hawk Trainer 3	Wards Motolympia
G–AKPG	Hawk Trainer 3	Wolverhampton Flying School
G–AKPH	Auster 5	N. B. Ewing
G–AKPI	Auster 5	J. F. Onions
G–AKPJ	Auster 5	D. Everall
G–AKPL	Hawk Trainer 3	Eagle Aviation

Registration	Type	Owner or Operator
G-AKPM	Hawk Trainer 3	W/Cmdr. H. C. Kennard
G-AKPX	Argus	R. L. Whyham
G-AKRC	Auster 5	J. Nicholson
G-AKRD	Ambassador	M.o.S.
G-AKRF	Sea Otter	R. L. Whyham
G-AKRG	Sea Otter	R. L. Whyham
G-AKRH	Hawk Trainer 3	S. J. Bartlam
G-AKRM	Hawk Trainer 3	B. A. G. Woodwards
G-AKRN	Dragon Rapide	East Anglian Flying Services
G-AKRO	Dragon Rapide	Inter-City Air Services
G-AKRP	Dragon Rapide	Short Bros. & Harland
G-AKRR	Dragon Rapide	Short Bros. & Harland
G-AKRS	Dragon Rapide	Air Enterprises
G-AKRT	Hawk Trainer 3	Short Bros. & Harland
G-AKRU	Hawk Trainer 3	Short Bros. & Harland
G-AKRV	Hawk Trainer 3	E. Day
G-AKRW	Hawk Trainer 3	Short Bros. & Harland
G-AKRX	Sea Otter	B.O.A.C.
G-AKSC	Dragon Rapide	Demolition & Construction
G-AKSD	Dragon Rapide	Windmill Theatre Transport Co.
G-AKSE	Dragon Rapide	Manx Air Charter
G-AKSG	Dragon Rapide	R. L. Whyham
G-AKSH	Dragon Rapide	Brooklands Aviation
G-AKSI	Auster 5	British Air Transport
G-AKSJ	Auster 5	
G-AKSK	Dove I	Olley Air Services
G-AKSL	Dragon Rapide	Goodhew Aviation
G-AKSM	Dakota 3	Sivewright Airways
G-AKSN	Lancastrian 2	Skyways Sky Consort
G-AKSO	Lancastrian 2	Skyways Sky Kingdom
G-AKSS	Dove I	British Air Transport
G-AKST	Dove I	Skyways
G-AKSV	Dove I	de Havilland Aircraft Co.
G-AKSW	Dove 2	Enfield Rolling Mills
G-AKSY	Auster 5	P. H. I. Jones
G-AKSZ	Auster 5	A. Robinson
G-AKTA	Auster 5	J. D. Hamilton
G-AKTB	Lancastrian 2	Flight Refuelling
G-AKTD	Dragon Rapide	Air Couriers
G-AKTF	Auster 5	Lancashire Aircraft Corp.
G-AKTU	Viking IB	Airwork
G-AKTV	Viking IB	Airwork
G-AKTW	Westland S–51	Westland Aircraft
G-AKTX	Dragon Rapide	Mayfair Air Services
G-AKTY	Dragon Rapide	Herts & Essex Aero Club
G-AKTZ	Dragon Rapide	Airwork
G-AKUA	Hawk Trainer 3	Fairey Aviation Co.
G-AKUB	Dragon Rapide	J. H. Watts & Ptns.
G-AKUC	Dragon Rapide	S. K. Davies
G-AKUD	Avro 19	M.o.S.
G-AKUS	Dragon Rapide	Mayfair Air Services
G-AKUV	Super Ace	Chrislea Aircraft Co.
G-AKUW	Super Ace	F. G. Ford (Estates)
G-AKUX	Super Ace	Enterprise Aviation Services
G-AKVA	Super Ace	Autowork (Winchester)

Registration	Type	Owner or Operator
G–AKVB	Super Ace	Chrislea Aircraft Co.
G–AKVC	Super Ace	Chrislea Aircraft Co.
G–AKVD	Super Ace	Autocars (Worcs.)
G–AKVE	Super Ace	Chrislea Aircraft Co.
G–AKVF	Super Ace	Chrislea Aircraft Co.
G–AKVG	Super Ace	Chrislea Aircraft Co.
G–AKVH	Super Ace	Chrislea Aircraft Co.
G–AKVI	Super Ace	Chrislea Aircraft Co.
G–AKVJ	Super Ace	Chrislea Aircraft Co.
G–AKVK	Super Ace	Chrislea Aircraft Co.
G–AKVL	Super Ace	Chrislea Aircraft Co.
G–AKVM	Super Ace	Chrislea Aircraft Co.
G–AKVN	Super Ace	Chrislea Aircraft Co.
G–AKVO	Super Ace	Chrislea Aircraft Co.
G–AKVP	Super Ace	Chrislea Aircraft Co.
G–AKVR	Super Ace	Chrislea Aircraft Co.
G–AKVS	Skyjeep	Chrislea Aircraft Co.
G–AKVT	Super Ace	Chrislea Aircra't Co.
G–AKVU	Dragon Rapide	Patrick Motors
G–AKVV	Proctor I	D. Goldstein
G–AKVW	Anson I	British Air Transport
G–AKVZ	Messenger 4A	Thomas Ratcliffe & Co.
G–AKWA	Sea Otter 2	B.O.A.C.
G–AKWE	Proctor 3	C. M. Chown
G–AKWF	Proctor 3	Morton Air Services
G–AKWH	Auster 5	Miss B. L. Duthy
G–AKWI	Auster 5	British Air Transport
G–AKWJ	Proctor 3	A. L. McLeod
G–AKWK	Auster 5	Furze Hill Laboratories
G–AKWL	Proctor 4	Southend Municipal Council
G–AKWM	Proctor 3	Aikman Airways
G–AKWN	Proctor 3	Aikman Airways
G–AKWO	Proctor 3	Lord Malcolm Douglas-Hamilton
G–AKWP	Proctor 3	Aikman Airways
G–AKWR	Proctor 3	Aikman Airways
G–AKWS	Auster 5	R. G. Banks
G–AKWT	Auster 5	V. G. Manton
G–AKWU	Proctor 3	International Air Exports
G–AKWV	Proctor 3	J. P. Crowther
G–AKWY	Tiger Moth	Isle of Wight Flying Club
G–AKXC	Tiger Moth	B. J. Doyle
G–AKXD	Tiger Moth	Mrs. L. K. King
G–AKXG	Tiger Moth	W. A. Rollason
G–AKXH	Tiger Moth	Surrey Financial Trust
G–AKXI	Proctor 3	G. M. Bowles-Evans
G–AKXJ	Proctor 3	E. R. Hill
G–AKXK	Proctor 3	Inter-City Air Services
G–AKXL	Proctor 3	Surrey Financial Trust
G–AKXO	Tiger Moth	Midland Aero Club
G–AKXP	Auster 5	Air Service Training
G–AKXR	Auster 5	Air Service Training
G–AKXS	Tiger Moth	Air Service Training
G–AKXT	Halifax 8	Lancashire Aircraft Corp.
G–AKXU	Tiger Moth	Air Service Training
G–AKXV	Tiger Moth	Air Service Training
G–AKXW	Anson I	Air Service Training
G–AKXZ	Proctor 3	P. W. Bayliss
G–AKYA	Proctor 5	Percival Aircraft

Registration	Type	Owner or Operator
G-AKYB	Proctor 5	Lancashire Aircraft Corp.
G-AKYC	Proctor 5	L. S. Dawson
G-AKYD	Proctor 5	Gloster Aircraft Co.
G-AKYG	Proctor 3	R. L. Whyham
G-AKYH	Sea Otter	R. L. Whyham
G-AKYJ	Proctor 4	Lancashire Aircraft Corp.
G-AKYK	Proctor 4	Lancashire Aircraft Corp.
G-AKYL	Tiger Moth	Scottish Flying Club
G-AKYM	Tiger Moth	Scottish Flying Club
G-AKYN	Tiger Moth	Adie Aviation
G-AKYP	Tiger Moth	Adie Aviation
G-AKYR	Tiger Moth	Cardiff Aeroplane Club
G-AKYS	Dove 2	David Brown & Sons (Huddersfield)
G-AKYT	Auster 5	C. G. Wheatley
G-AKYU	Auster 5	H. Mitchell
G-AKZB	Dragon Rapide	B.E.A.C.
G-AKZC	Messenger 4A	Wolverhampton Aviation
G-AKZD	Proctor 3	
G-AKZE	Proctor 3	R. L. Whyham
G-AKZF	Proctor 3	R. L. Whyham
G-AKZG	Proctor 3	D. E. Barton
G-AKZH	Dragon Rapide	Herts & Essex Aero Club
G-AKZI	Dragon Rapide	Mayfai rAir Services
G-AKZJ	Dragon Rapide	Mediterranean Air Services
G-AKZK	Tiger Moth	Air Service Training
G-AKZL	Tiger Moth	Air Service Training
G-AKZM	Tiger Moth	Air Service Training
G-AKZN	Proctor 3	Air Service Training
G-AKZO	Dragon Rapide	J. Nesbit-Evans & Co.
G-AKZP	Dragon Rapide	E. Holden
G-AKZR	Proctor 3	Hyland Ltd.
G-AKZS	Proctor 3	Hyland Ltd.
G-AKZT	Dragon Rapide	R. L. Whyham
G-AKZU	Messenger 4A	Morgan Aviation
G-AKZW	Dragon Rapide	H. A. E. Towle
G-AKZX	Messenger 4A	N. M. Browning
G-AKZY	Me 108 D–I	Air Couriers
G-AKZZ	Messenger 4A	N. M. Browning
G-ALAA	Proctor 5	Percival Aircraft
G-ALAB	Proctor 5	Percival Aircraft
G-ALAC	Proctor 5	Percival Aircraft
G-ALAD	Proctor 5	Percival Aircraft
G-ALAE	Messenger 4A	E. W. Wagner
G-ALAF	Messenger 4A	E. J. Morton
G-ALAG	Messenger 4A	J. C. Rice
G-ALAH	Messenger 4A	E. P. Jenks
G-ALAI	Messenger 4A	L. W. Hamp
G-ALAJ	Messenger 4A	L. W. Farrer
G-ALAK	Constellation	B.O.A.C. *Brentford*
G-ALAL	Constellation	B.O.A.C. *Banbury*
G-ALAM	Constellation	B.O.A.C. *Belfast*
G-ALAN	Constellation	B.O.A.C. *Beaufort*
G-ALAO	Constellation	B.O.A.C. *Braemar*
G-ALAP	Messenger 4A	Porter Spiers (Leics.)
G-ALAR	Messenger 4A	T. W. Leadbetter
G-ALAT	Dragon Rapide	J. H. Watts & Ptns.
G-ALAV	Messenger 4A	N. B. Neaum
G-ALAW	Messenger 4A	Skegness Steam Laundry Co.

Registration	Type	Owner or Operator
G–ALAX	Dragon Rapide	Saunders-Roe
G–ALBA	Dragon Rapide	R. A. Gunton
G–ALBB	Dragon Rapide	E. A. Taylor
G–ALBC	Dragon Rapide	M. H. D. McAlpine
G–ALBD	Tiger Moth	College of Aeronautics
G–ALBE	Messenger 4A	E. W. Westbrook
G–ALBF	Dove I	Iraq Petroleum Transport Co.
G–ALBH	Dragon Rapide	Scottish Aviation
G–ALBJ	Auster 5	V. G. Manton
G–ALBK	Auster 5	V. G. Manton
G–ALBL	Primer	Fairey Aviation Co.
G–ALBM	Dove I	de Havilland Aircraft Co.
G–ALBN	Bristol 173	M.o.S.
G–ALBO	Bristol 175	Bristol Aeroplane Co.
G–ALBP	Messenger 4A	J. E. Nicholson
G–ALBS	Halifax 8	Hyland Automobiles
G–ALBT	Halifax 8	Hyland Automobiles
G–ALBU	Halifax 8	Hyland Automobiles
G–ALBV	Halifax 8	Hyland Automobiles
G–ALBW	Auster 5	Photoflight
G–ALCB	Dakota 3	B.E.A.C.
G–ALCC	Dakota 3	B.E.A.C.
G–ALCD	Dakota 3	
G–ALCH	Proctor 3	Lancashire Aircraft Corp.
G–ALCJ	Proctor 3	Lancashire Aircraft Corp.
G–ALCK	Proctor 3	Lancashire Aircraft Corp.
G–ALCL	Proctor 3	W. Jamison
G–ALCM	Prince I	Percival Aircraft
G–ALCN	Proctor 3	R. Watson
G–ALCO	Proctor 3	
G–ALCP	Proctor 3	
G–ALCR	Proctor 3	C. W. J. Allen
G–ALCS	Gemini 3A	Claremont Shipping Co.
G–ALCT	Auster 5	
G–ALCU	Dove 2	E. P. Jenks Ltd.
G–ALCW	Air Horse	M.o.S.
G–ALCX	Halifax 8	Lancashire Aircraft Corp.
G–ALCY	Halifax 3	
G–ALCZ	Halifax 3	
G–ALDA	Hermes 4	B.O.A.C. Hecuba
G–ALDB	Hermes 4	B.O.A.C. Hebe
G–ALDC	Hermes 4	B.O.A.C. Hermione
G–ALDD	Hermes 4	B.O.A.C. Hannibal
G–ALDE	Hermes 4	B.O.A.C. Hanno
G–ALDF	Hermes 4	B.O.A.C. Hadrian
G–ALDG	Hermes 4	B.O.A.C. Horsa
G–ALDH	Hermes 4	B.O.A.C. Heracles
G–ALDI	Hermes 4	B.O.A.C. Horatius
G–ALDJ	Hermes 4	B.O.A.C. Hengist
G–ALDK	Hermes 4	B.O.A.C. Helena
G–ALDL	Hermes 4	B.O.A.C. Hector
G–ALDM	Hermes 4	B.O.A.C. Hero
G–ALDN	Hermes 4	B.O.A.C. Horus
G–ALDO	Hermes 4	B O.A.C. Heron
G–ALDP	Hermes 4	B.O.A.C. Homer
G–ALDR	Hermes 4	B.O.A.C. Herodotus
G–ALDS	Hermes 4	B.O.A.C. Hesperides
G–ALDT	Hermes 4	B.O.A.C. Hesta

Registration	Type	Owner or Operator
G-ALDU	Hermes 4	B.O.A.C. *Halcyone*
G-ALDV	Hermes 4	B.O.A.C. *Hera*
G-ALDW	Hermes 4	B.O.A.C. *Helios*
G-ALDX	Hermes 4	B.O.A.C. *Hyperion*
G-ALDY	Hermes 4	B.O.A.C. *Honor*
G-ALDZ	Halifax 3	
G-ALEA	Halifax 3	
G-ALEB	Halifax 3	
G-ALEC	Halifax 3	
G-ALED	Halifax 3	
G-ALEE	Halifax 3	
G-ALEF	Halifax 8	Eagle Aviation
G-ALEG	Westland S.51/1A	Pest Control
G-ALEI	Westland S.51/1	Pest Control
G-ALEJ	Dragon Rapide	Lancashire Aircraft Corp.
G-ALEM	Anson 1	
G-ALEN	Anson 1	
G-ALEO	Proctor 4	
G-ALEP	Skymaster	Mining & Exploration Air Services
G-ALER	Proctor 3	R. C. Preston
G-ALES	Proctor 3	
G-ALET	Dragon Rapide	Mannin Airways
G-ALEU	Hermes 5	M.o.S.
G-ALEV	Hermes 5	M.o.S.
G-ALEX	Proctor 4	
G-ALEY	Auster 5	J. M. Sykes
G-ALEZ	Dakota	
G-ALFA	Auster 5	A. Harrison
G-ALFB	Proctor 3	Silver City Airways
G-ALFC	Proctor 3	
G-ALFD	Anson	
G-ALFE	Hawk Trainer 3	H. J. C. Turner
G-ALFF	Proctor 3	G. Cribb
G-ALFG	Tiger Moth	Short Bros. & Harland
G-ALFH	Hawk Trainer 3	Airways Aero Assoc.
G-ALFI	Hawk Trainer 3	Airways Aero Assoc.
G-ALFK	Proctor 3	C. M. Chown
G-ALFN	Avro 19/2	Secretary of State for Air
G-ALFO	Dakota 3	The Zinc Corporation
G-ALFP	Anson 1	Finglands Airways
G-ALFR	Ambassador	Airspeed Ltd.
G-ALFS	Proctor 3	B. H. Hurle-Hobbs
G-ALFT	Dove 2	M.C.A.
G-ALFU	Dove 2	M.C.A.
G-ALFV	Proctor 3	
G-ALFW	Proctor 3	
G-ALFX	Proctor 3	Autocars (Worcs.)
G-ALFY	Proctor 3	
G-ALFZ	Prince 1	Percival Aircraft
G-ALGA	Kirby Kitten	Airways Aero Assoc.
G-ALGB	Dragon Rapide 2	R. H. Braime & Ptns.
G-ALGC	Dragon Rapide 2	A. R. Pilgrim
G-ALGE	Dragon Rapide 2	Melba Airways
G-ALGG	Proctor 3	
G-ALGH	J-3C Cub	H. Tinsley

Registration	Type	Owner or Operator
G–ALGI	Dragon Rapide 2	W. Westoby
G–ALGJ	Hawk Trainer 3	W. L. Foster
G–ALGK	Hawk Trainer 3	Short Bros. & Harland
G–ALGL	Proctor 4	R. L. Whyham
G–ALGM	Dragon Rapide	Adie Aviation
G–ALGN	Dragon Rapide	Adie Aviation
G–ALGO	Dragon Rapide	Anglo-Iranian Oil Co.
G–ALGP	Proctor 3	Adie Aviation
G–ALGR	Proctor 3	Adie Aviation
G–ALGS	Proctor 3	G. P. Reece
G–ALGT	Spitfire 14	Rolls-Royce
G–ALGU	Mosquito 19	Flight Refuelling
G–ALGV	Mosquito 19	Flight Refuelling
G–ALGW	Auster 6	K. V. Nelson
G–ALGX	Tiger Moth	H. B. Showell
G–ALGY	Proctor 3	T. G. Henderson
G–ALGZ	Hawk Trainer 3	Sqdn. Ldr. Nalson
G–ALHA	Hawk Trainer 3	Sqdn. Ldr. Nalson
G–ALHB	Hawk Trainer 3	Sqdn. Ldr. Nalson
G–ALHC	Canadair Four	B.O.A.C. *Ariadne*
G–ALHD	Canadair Four	B.O.A.C. *Ajax*
G–ALHE	Canadair Four	B.O.A.C. *Argo*
G–ALHF	Canadair Four	B.O.A.C. *Atlas*
G–ALHG	Canadair Four	B.O.A.C. *Aurora*
G–ALHH	Canadair Four	B.O.A.C. *Attica*
G–ALHI	Canadair Four	B.O.A.C. *Antares*
G–ALHJ	Canadair Four	B.O.A.C. *Arcturus*
G–ALHK	Canadair Four	B.O.A.C. *Atalanta*
G–ALHL	Canadair Four	B.O.A.C. *Altair*
G–ALHM	Canadair Four	B.O.A.C. *Antaeus*
G–ALHN	Canadair Four	B.O.A.C. *Argosy*
G–ALHO	Canadair Four	B.O.A.C. *Amazon*
G–ALHP	Canadair Four	B.O.A.C. *Aethra*
G–ALHR	Canadair Four	B.O.A.C. *Antiope*
G–ALHS	Canadair Four	B.O.A.C. *Astra*
G–ALHT	Canadair Four	B.O.A.C. *Athena*
G–ALHU	Canadair Four	B.O.A.C. *Artemis*
G–ALHV	Canadair Four	B.O.A.C. *Adonis*
G–ALHW	Canadair Four	B.O.A.C. *Aeolus*
G–ALHX	Canadair Four	B.O.A.C. *Astroea*
G–ALHY	Canadair Four	B.O.A.C. *Arion*
G–ALHZ	Anson 10	R. L. Whyham
G–ALIA	Anson 10	R. L. Whyham
G–ALIB	Anson 10	R. L. Whyham
G–ALIC	Anson 10	R. L. Whyham
G–ALID	Anson 11	R. L. Whyham
G–ALIE	Anson 11	R. L. Whyham
G–ALIF	Anson 11	R. L. Whyham
G–ALIG	Anson 11	R. L. Whyham
G–ALIH	Anson 11	R. L. Whyham
G–ALII	Anson 11	R. L. Whyham
G–ALIJ	Seaford	R. L. Whyham
G–ALIK	Westland S.51/1A	Westland Aircraft
G–ALIM	Hawk Trainer 3	Short Bros. & Harland
G–ALIN	Hawk Trainer 3	Short Bros. & Harland
G–ALIO	Hawk Trainer 3	Maj. Gen. J. E. C. McCandlish
G–ALIP	Hawk Trainer 3	Short Bros. & Harland
G–ALIR	Halifax 9	Aviation Traders

Registration	Type	Owner or Operator
G–ALIS	Proctor 3	W. A. Stuart
G–ALIT	Proctor 3	B. C. Barton & Son
G–ALIU	Tiger Moth	Wolverhampton Flying Club
G–ALIV	Tiger Moth	Wolverhampton Flying Club
G–ALIX	Tiger Moth	London Aeroplane Club
G–ALIY	Tiger Moth	Derby Aviation
G–ALJA	Prince 1	Percival Aircraft
G–ALJB	Auster 5	A. E. Morris
G–ALJC	Auster 5	Darlington & District Aero Club
G–ALJD	Auster 5	Darlington & District Aero Club
G–ALJE	Auster 4	Darlington & District Aero Club
G–ALJF	Proctor 3	Darlington & District Aero Club
G–ALJH	Proctor 3	S. N. Dennis
G–ALJI	Proctor 3	Central Aeronautical Bureau
G–ALJJ	Beech Model 18S	
G–ALJK	Proctor 3	L. K. Jackson
G–ALJL	Tiger Moth	Air Service Training
G–ALKA	Auster	
G–ALKB	Auster	
G–ALKC	Auster	
G–ALKD	Auster	
G–ALKE	Auster	
G–ALKF	Auster	
G–ALKG	Auster	
G–ALKH	Auster	
G–ALKI	Auster 5C	A. H. Wheeler
G–ALKK	Auster 5	
G–ALKL	Westland S–51	Westland Aircraft
G–ALLI	Dakota 3	B.E.A.C.
G–ALLK	Drover	de Havilland Aircraft Co.
G–ALMA	J–3C Cub	E. N. Haywood
G–ALMB	Westland S–51	Westland Aircraft
G–ALMC	Westland S–51	Westland Aircraft
G–ALMD	Westland S–51	Westland Aircraft
G–ALMR	Dove 2	de Havilland Aircraft Co.
G–ALMS	Proctor 3	T. A. Menzies
G–ALNA	Tiger Moth	Bembridge and Sandown Aero Club
G–ALND	Tiger Moth	Air Service Training
G–ALNS	Dragon Rapide	W. Hutchinson
G–ALNT	Dragon Rapide	W. Hutchinson
G–ALNU	Auster 5	
G–ALNV	Auster 5	Tattersalls Garages
G–ALNW	Auster 5	
G–ALNX	Hawk Trainer 3	R. A. Short
G–ALNY	Hawk Trainer 3	R. A. Short
G–ALNZ	Hawk Trainer 3	R. A. Short
G–ALOA	Hawk Trainer 3	R. A. Short
G–ALOB	Hawk Trainer 3	R. A. Short
G–ALOC	Hawk Trainer 3	R. A. Short
G–ALOE	Hawk Trainer 3	R. A. Short
G–ALOF	Hawk Trainer 3	R. A. Short
G–ALOG	Hawk Trainer 3	D. M. Brown
G–ALOH	Hawk Trainer 3	
G–ALOI	Satellite	Planet Aircraft
G–ALOJ	Proctor	
G–ALOK	Proctor 3	Miss B. John
G–ALOL	Proctor	
G–ALOM	Halifax 6	Aviation Traders

Above : Percival PROCTOR.
Best-known of the excellent
Percival sporting and touring
'planes, the Proctor is a
comfortable, high-perform-
ance four-seater, widely used
both privately and by the
R.A.F.

Right : Aeronca 100. One of
the smallest British aircraft,
the ultra-light Aeronca 100
is powered by a 36 h.p.
J.A.P. engine (John W. R.
Taylor.)

Below : Vickers SPITFIRE
TRAINER. Two-seat training
version of the famous Spitfire
fighter. G–AIDN is Vickers'
demonstration model. (F. G.
Swanborough.)

Top : Sopwith PUP. Oldest aircraft on the register, this Sopwith Pup, built in 1916, is still used in aerobatic displays.

Centre : de Havilland TIGER MOTH. Most of the R.A.F.'s wartime pilots completed their early training on "Tigers," which are still used extensively for sporting and club flying.

Bottom : Miles MESSENGER. Single-engined counterpart of the Gemini, which was developed from the Messenger. Both aircraft feature prominent high-lift wing flaps, which enable them to land and take off in restricted spaces.

Registration	Type	Owner or Operator
G–ALON	Halifax 9	Aviation Traders
G–ALOS	Halifax 9	Aviation Traders
G–ALOU	Bristol 171/1	M.o.S.
G–ALOV	Dragon Rapide	Short Bros. & Harland
G–ALOW	Beaver	de Havilland Aircraft Co.
G–ALOX	Tiger Moth	Airways Aero. Assoc.
G–ALPF	Lincoln 2	Airtech
G–ALPK	Dragon Rapide	Lancashire Aircraft Corp.
G–ALPM	Douglas DC–3	
G–ALPN	Douglas DC–3	
G–ALRW	Dragon Rapide	Cambrian Air Services
G–ALRX	Bristol 175	Bristol Aeroplane Co.
G–ALRY	Prince P.54	Hunting Aerosurveys
G–ALSA	Stratocruiser	B.O.A.C. *Cathay*
G–ALSB	Stratocruiser	B.O.A.C. *Champion*
G–ALSC	Stratocruiser	B.O.A.C. *Centaurus*
G–ALSD	Stratocruiser	B.O.A.C. *Cassiopeia*
G–ALSH	Tiger Moth	Wiltshire School of Flying
G–ALSK	Halifax 9	Aviation Traders
G–ALSL	Halifax 9	Aviation Traders
G–ALSM	Proctor 3	L. W. Watkins
G–ALSP	Bristol 171/3	Bristol Aeroplane Co
G–ALSR	Bristol 171/3	Bristol Aeroplane Co.
G–ALSS	Bristol 171/3	Bristol Aeroplane Co.
G–ALST	Bristol 171/3	Bristol Aeroplane Co.
G–ALSU	Bristol 171/3	Bristol Aeroplane Co.
G–ALSV	Bristol 171/3	Bristol Aeroplane Co.
G–ALSW	Bristol 171/3	Bristol Aeroplane Co.
G–ALSX	Bristol 171/3	Bristol Aeroplane Co.
G–ALSY	Bristol 171/3	Bristol Aeroplane Co.
G–ALSZ	Bristol 171/3	Bristol Aeroplane Co.
G–ALTA	Bristol 171/3	Bristo! Aeroplane Co.
G–ALTB	Bristol 171/3	Bristol Aeroplane Co.
G–ALTC	Bristol 171/3	Bristol Aeroplane Co.
G–ALTD	Bristol 171/3	Bristol Aeroplane Co.
G–ALTE	Bristol 171/3	Bristol Aeroplane Co.
G–ALTF	Proctor 3	
G–ALTG	Proctor 3	
G–ALTM	Dove 2	B.O.A.C.
G–ALTP	Oxford 1	Air Service Training
G–ALTR	Oxford 1	Air Service Training
G–ALTT	Dakota 3	B.E.A.C.
G–ALTW	Tiger Moth	F. B. Scott
G–ALTX	Sea Otter	
G–ALTZ	Consul	B.O.A.C. *Star Monitor*
G–ALUA	Zaunkoenig	U.L.A.A.
G–ALUB	Marathon 1	Handley Page (Reading)
G–ALUC	Tiger Moth	W. A. Webb
G–ALUE	Autocrat	J. M. Heathcoty
G–ALUF	Skeeter 2	Cierva Autogiro Co.
G–ALUG	Gemini 1A	J. P. G. Daly
G–ALUI	Proctor 3	
G–ALUJ	Proctor 3	
G–ALUK	Proctor 3	
G–ALUM	Anson 1	Transair
G–ALUN	Princess	M.o.S.
G–ALUO	Princess	M.o.S.
G–ALUP	Princess	M.o.S.

Registration	Type	Owner or Operator
G–ALUR	Anson I	Aviation Traders
G–ALUS	Anson I	Aviation Traders
G–ALUT	Halifax 9	Aviation Traders
G–ALUU	Halifax 9	Aviation Traders
G–ALUV	Halifax 9	Aviation Traders
G–ALUW	Hawk Trainer 3	W. A. Rollason
G–ALUX	Hawk Trainer 3	W. A. Rollason
G–ALUY	Proctor 3	
G–ALUZ	Luton Minor	
G–ALVA	Proctor 3	
G–ALVC	Lancaster 7	Eagle Aviation
G–ALVD	Dove 2	Dunlop Rubber Co.
G–ALVE	Proctor 3	
G–ALVF	Lodestar	
G–ALVG	Comet	M.o.S.
G–ALVP	Tiger Moth	R. Pointer
G–ALVR	J–3C Cub	A. J. Walter
G–ALVS	Dove 2	M.C.A.
G–ALVT	Dove 2	M.C.A.
G–ALVU	Dragon Rapide	C. G. S. Whyham
G–ALVV	Auster 5	C. G. S. Whyham
G–ALVW	Marathon I	Handley Page (Reading)
G–ALVX	Marathon I	Handley Page (Reading)
G–ALVY	Marathon I	Handley Page (Reading)
G–ALVZ	Dakota	Crewsair
G–ALWA	Athena 2	M.o.S.
G–ALWB	Chipmunk	de Havilland Aircraft Co.
G–ALWC	Dakota 3	Airtech
G–ALWD	Dakota 3	Airtech
G–ALWE	Viscount	Vickers-Armstrongs
G–ALWF	Viscount	Vickers-Armstrongs
G–ALWI	Dragon Rapide	Short Bros. & Harland
G–ALWJ	Dragon Rapide	Short Bros. & Harland
G–ALWK	Dragon Rapide	R. C. Cox
G–ALWL	Dragon Rapide	V. H. Bellamy
G–ALWM	Dragon Rapide	V. H. Bellamy
G–ALWN	Dragon Rapide	V. H. Bellamy
G–ALWO	Dragon Rapide	Wealey & Nash
G–ALWP	Dragon Rapide	Allen Aircraft Services
G–ALWR	Proctor I	Air Service Training
G–ALWS	Tiger Moth	Air Service Training
G–ALWT	Tiger Moth	Air Service Training
G–ALWU	Tiger Moth	Air Service Training
G–ALWV	Tiger Moth	Air Service Training
G–ALWW	Tiger Moth	Air Service Training
G–ALWX	Anson	Air Enterprises
G–ALWY	Dragon Rapide	Air Enterprises
G–ALXA	Dragon Rapide	Darlington & Dist. Aero Club
G–ALXB	Anson I	Transair
G–ALXC	Anson I	Transair
G–ALXD	Anson I	Transair
G–ALXE	Anson I	Transair
G–ALXF	Anson I	Mrs. D. Whyham
G–ALXG	Anson I	Mrs. D. Whyham
G–ALXH	Anson I	Mrs. D. Whyham

Registration	Type	Owner or Operator
G–ALXI	Dragon Rapide	Mrs. D. Whyham
G–ALXJ	Dragon Rapide	Mrs. D Whyham
G–ALXK	Dakota 4	B.E.A.C.
G–ALXL	Dakota 4	B.E.A.C.
G–ALXM	Dakota 4	B.E.A.C.
G–ALXN ⎱ G–ALXO ⎰	Dakota 3	Scottish Aviation
G–ALXP	Firth Helicopter	Firth Helicopters
G–ALXR	Marathon I	Handley Page (Reading)
G–ALXS	Dragon Rapide	R. A. Short
G–ALXT	Dragon Rapide	A. R. Frogley
G–ALXU	Dragon Rapide	R. A. Short
G–ALXX	Oxford	Lancashire Aircraft Corp.
G–ALXY	Oxford	Lancashire Aircraft Corp.
G–ALXZ	Auster 5	S. J. Cooper
G–ALYA	Herald	Hants & Sussex Aviation
G–ALYB	Auster 5	L .R. Vandome
G–ALYC	Proctor I	D. E. Bianchi
G–ALYD	Auster 5	D. G. S. Cotter
G–ALYE	Anson I	Transair
G–ALYF	Dakota 3	Scottish Aviation
G–ALYG		
G–ALYH	Auster 5	T. H. Marshall
G–ALYO	Devon 1	Secretary of State for Air
G–ALZE	Britten-Norman B.N.—F.1.	
G–ALZF	Dragon Rapide	
G–ALZG	Gemini IA	P. Blamire
G–ALZH	Dragon Rapide	W. J. E. Lee
G–ALZJ	Dragon Rapide	Cambrian Air Services
G–ALZK	Comet	M.o.S.
G–ALZL	Heron	de Havilland Aircraft Co.
G–AMAI	Dragon Rapide	
G–AMAJ	Tiger Moth	
G–AMAK	Westland S.51	
G–AMAL	Proctor I	
G–AMAM	Dragon Rapide	
G–AMAN	Proctor I	
G–AMAO	Auster 5	
G–AMAP	Auster 5	J. Green
G–AMAR	Tiger Moth	
G–AMAU	Hurricane 2c	Hawker Aircraft Ltd.
G–AMBE	Anson I	
G–AMBF	Anson I	
G–AMBG	Anson I	
G–AMBH	Gemini IA	E. G. Hayes
G–AMBI	Tiger Moth	
G–AMBJ	Tiger Moth	
G–AMBK	Tiger Moth	
G–AMBS	Proctor 3	
G–AMBT	Consul	Airspeed
G–AMBU	Consul	Airspeed
G–AMBW	Dakota 3	Airwork
G–AMBX	Halifax 9	
G–AMCA	Dakota	
G–AMCF	Halifax 9	
G–AMCG	Halifax 9	

Foreign Air Liners
Serving the U.K.

In alphabetical order

CANADA (CF)

Registration	Type	Owner or Operator
CF–TFA	North Star	Trans-Canada Air Lines
CF–TFB	,, ,,	,, ,, ,, ,,
CF–TFC	,, ,,	,, ,, ,, ,,
CF–TFD	,, ,,	,, ,, ,, ,,
CF–TFE	,, ,,	,, ,, ,, ,,
CF–TFF	,, ,,	,, ,, ,, ,,
CF–TFG	,, ,,	,, ,, ,, ,,
CF–TFH	,, ,,	,, ,, ,, ,,
CF–TFI	,, ,,	,, ,, ,, ,,
CF–TFJ	,, ,,	,, ,, ,, ,,
CF–TFK	,, ,,	,, ,, ,, ,,
CF–TFL	,, ,,	,, ,, ,, ,,
CF–TFM	,, ,,	,, ,, ,, ,,
CF–TFN	,, ,,	,, ,, ,, ,,
CF–TFO	,, ,,	,, ,, ,, ,,
CF–TFP	,, ,,	,, ,, ,, ,,
CF–TFQ	,, ,,	,, ,, ,, ,,
CF–TFR	,, ,,	,, ,, ,, ,,
CF–TFS	,, ,,	,, ,, ,, ,,
CF–TFT	,, ,,	,, ,, ,, ,,

PORTUGAL (CS)

Registration	Type	Owner or Operator
CS–TSA	Douglas DC–4	Transportes Aereos Portugueses
CS–TSB	,, ,,	,, ,, ,,
CS–TSD	,, ,,	,, ,, ,,

SPAIN (EC)

Registration	Type	Owner or Operator
EC–ACD	Douglas DC–4	Iberia
EC–ACE	,, ,,	,,
EC–ACF	,, ,,	,,
EC–AEK	,, ,,	,,
EC–AEO	,, ,,	,,
EC–AEP	,, ,,	,,

EIRE (EI)

Registration	Type	Owner or Operator
EI–ACD	Douglas C–47	Aer Lingus St. Patrick
EI–ACE	Douglas DC–3D	,, ,, St. Colmcille
EI–ACF	Douglas DC–3D	,, ,, St. Kieran
EI–ACG	Douglas C–47	,, ,, St. Malachy
EI–ACH	Douglas C–47A	,, ,, St. Brigid
EI–ACI	Douglas C–47	,, ,, St. Aidan
EI–ACK	Douglas C–47A	,, ,, St. Albert
EI–ACL	Douglas C–47	,, ,, St. Declan
EI–ACM	Douglas C–47	,, ,, St. Fintan
EI–ACT	Douglas C–47A	,, ,, St. Colman
EI–AFA.	Douglas C–47A	,, ,, St. Kevin
EI–AFB	Douglas C–47A	,, ,, St. Brendan
EI–AFC	Douglas DC–3F	,, ,, St. Enda

FRANCE (F)

Registration	Type	Owner or Operator
F–BATA	Languedoc	Air France
F–BATB	,,	,, ,,
F–BATC	,,	,, ,,
F–BATD	,,	,, ,,
F–BATE	,,	,, ,,
F–BATG	,,	,, ,,
F–BATH	,,	,, ,,
F–BATI	,,	,, ,,
F–BATJ	,,	,, ,,
F–BATK	,,	,, ,,
F–BATL	,,	,, ,,
F–BATN	,,	,, ,,
F–BATO	,,	,, ,,
F–BATP	,,	,, ,,
F–BATQ	,,	,, ,,
F–BATR	,,	,, ,,
F–BATS	,,	,, ,,
F–BATT	,,	,, ,,
F–BATU	,,	,, ,,
F–BATV	,,	,, ,,
F–BATW	,,	,, ,,
F–BATX	,,	,, ,,
F–BATY	,,	,, ,,
F–BATZ	,,	,, ,,
F–BBDA	Douglas DC–4	,, ,, Ciel de Bretagne
F–BBDB	,, ,,	,, ,, Ciel de Touraine
F–BBDD	,, ,,	,, ,, Ciel de Bourgogne
F–BBDE	,, ,,	,, ,, Ciel de Picardie
F–BBDF	,, ,,	,, ,, Ciel de Artois
F–BBDG	,, ,,	,, ,, Ciel de Champagne
F–BBDH	,, ,,	,, ,, Ciel de Bearn
F–BBDI	,, ,,	,, ,, Ciel de Provence
F–BBDJ	,, ,,	,, ,, Ciel Ile de France
F–BBDK	,, ,,	,, ,, Ciel de Normandie

Registration	Type	Owner or Operator
F–BBDL	Douglas DC–4	Air France *Ciel de Alsace*
F–BBDM	,, ,,	,, ,, *Ciel de Gascogne*
F–BBDN	,, ,,	,, ,, *Ciel de Lorraine*
F–BBDO	,, ,,	,, ,, *Ciel de Savoie*
F–BBDP	,, ,,	,, ,,
F–BBDQ	,, ,,	,, ,,
F–BBDR	,, ,,	,, ,,
F–BCUA	Languedoc	,, ,,
F–BCUB	,,	,, ,,
F–BCUE	,,	,, ,,
F–BCUF	,,	,, ,,
F–BCUG	,,	,, ,,
F–BCUH	,,	,, ,,
F–BCUI	,,	,, ,,
F–BCUJ	,,	,, ,,
F–BCUK	,,	,, ,,
F–BCUL	,,	,, ,,
F–BCUM	,,	,, ,,
F–BCUN	,,	,, ,,
F–BCUO	,,	,, ,,
F–BCUP	,,	,, ,,
F–BCUR	,,	,, ,,
F–BCUS	,,	,, ,,
F–BELC	Douglas DC–4	,, ,,
F–BELD	,, ,,	,, ,,
F–BELE	,, ,,	,, ,,
F–BELF	,, ,,	,, ,,
F–BELI	,, ,,	,, ,,
F–BELJ	,, ,,	,, ,,
F–BELK	,, ,,	,, ,,
F–BELL	,, ,,	,, ,,
F–BELM	,, ,,	,, ,,
F–BELN	,, ,,	,, ,,

SWITZERLAND (HB)

HB–ILA	Douglas DC–4	Swissair *Geneve*
HB–ILE	,, ,,	,,
HB–ILI	,, ,,	,, *Basel*
HB–ILO	,, ,,	,,
HB–IRA	Douglas DC–3	,,
HB–IRB	,, ,,	,,
HB–IRC	,, ,,	,,
HB–IRD	,, ,,	,,
HB–IRE	,, ,,	,,
HB–IRF	,, ,,	,,
HB–IRG	,, ,,	,,
HB–IRI	,, ,,	,,
HB–IRK	,, ,,	,,
HB–IRL	,, ,,	,,
HB–IRM	,, ,,	,,
HB–IRN	,, ,,	,,
HB–IRO	,, ,,	,,

Registration	Type	Owner or Operator
HB–IRP	Convair-Liner	Swissair
HB–IRS	,, ,,	,,
HB–IRT	,, ,,	,,
HB–IRV	,, ,,	,,
HB–IRX	Douglas DC–3	,,

ITALY (I)

I-DALJ	S.I.A.I. Marchetti S.M.95	Alitalia *Christoforo Colombo*
I-DALK	,, ,, ,,	,, *Amerigo Vespucci*
I-DALL	,, ,, ,,	,, *Marco Polo*
I-DALN	,, ,, ,,	,, *Sebastiano Caboto*
I-DALO	,, ,, ,,	,, *Ugo Vivaldi*

NORWAY (LN)

LN–LAG	Douglas DC–6	Scandinavian Airlines System *Sverre*
LN–LAH	,, ,,	,, ,, ,, *Harald*

N.B.   Scandinavian Airlines System aircraft names are suffixed " **Viking** "

ARGENTINA (LV)

LV–AFV	York	F.A.M.A.
LV–AFY	York	,,
LV–AFZ	York	,,

LUXEMBOURG (LX)

LX–LAA	Douglas C–47	Luxembourg Airlines *Echternach*
LX–LAC	Dragon Rapide	,, ,,
LX–LAD	,, ,,	,, ,,

U.S.A. (N)

N1027V	Stratocruiser	P.A.A. *America*
N1028V	,,	,, *Flyin Cloud*

Registration	Type	Owner or Operator
N1031V	Stratocruiser	P.A.A. *Mayflower*
N1032V	,,	,, *United States*
N1033V	,,	,, *Seven Seas*
N1034V	,,	,, *Westward Ho !*
N1035V	,,	,, *Flying Eagle*
N1036V	,,	,, *Washington*
N1041V	,,	,,
N	,,	,,
N	,,	,,
N25686	Douglas DC–3	A.O.A. *Helsinki*
N88832	Constellation	P.A.A. *Flora Temple*
N88833	,,	,, *Robin Hood*
N88836	,,	,, *Yankee Ranger*
N88837	,,	,, *Challenge*
N88838	,,	,, *Donald McKay*
N88846	,,	,, *Great Republic*
N88847	,,	,, *Hotspur*
N88850	,,	,, *Intrepid*
N88855	,,	,, *Undaunted*
N88856	,,	,, *Paul Jones*
N88857	,,	,, *Flying Mist*
N88859	,,	,, *Talisman*
N88861	,,	,, *Winged Arrow*
N88868	,,	,, *Golden Fleece*
N88919	Douglas DC–4	,, *Panama*
N88922	,, ,,	,, *Radiant*
N88923	,, ,,	,, *West Wind*
N88926	,, ,,	,, *Twilight*
N88927	,, ,,	,, *Skylark*
N88933	,, ,,	,, *Winged Racer*
N88934	,, ,,	,, *Pride of America*
N88942	,, ,,	,, *Bostonian*
N88945	,, ,,	,, *Gladiator*
N88955	,, ,,	,, *Nonpareil*
N88958	,, ,,	,, *Derby*
N88959	,, ,,	,, *Live Yankee*
N90902	,, ,,	A.O.A. *Frankfurt*
N90905	,, ,,	,, *Berlin*
N90908	Douglas DC–3	,, *Nairobi*
N90913	Douglas DC–4	P.A.A.
N90921	Constellation	A.O.A. *London*
N90922	,,	,, *Oslo*
N90923	,,	,, *Stockholm*
N90924	,,	,, *Shannon*
N90925	,,	,, *Copenhagen*
N90926	,,	,, *Amsterdam*
N90927	,,	,, *Glasgow*
N90941	Stratocruiser	,, *Europe*
N90942	,,	,, *Great Britain*
N90943	,,	,, *Holland*
N90944	,,	,, *Ireland*
N90945	,,	,, *Norway*
N90946	,,	,, *Sweden*
N90947	,,	,, *Denmark*
N90948	,,	,, *Scotland*

N.B. P.A.A. aircraft names are prefixed **Clipper**
A.O.A.   ,,   ,,   ,,   ,,   **Flagship**

CZECHOSLOVAKIA (OK)

Registration	Type	Owner or Operator
OK–CBA	Ilyushin II 12	Cs Statni Aerolinie
OK–CBB	,, ,, ,,	,, ,, ,,
OK–CBC	,, ,, ,,	,, ,, ,,
OK–CBD	,, ,, ,,	,, ,, ,,
OK–CBE	,, ,, ,,	,, ,, ,,
OK–CBF	,, ,, ,,	,, ,, ,,
OK–CBG	,, ,, ,,	,, ,, ,,
OK–CBH	,, ,, ,,	,, ,, ,,
OK–CBJ	,, ,, ,,	,, ,, ,,
OK–CBK	,, ,, ,,	,, ,, ,,
OK–WAA	Douglas DC–3	,, ,, ,,
OK–WAP	,, ,,	,, ,, ,,
OK–WAX	,, ,,	,, ,, ,,
OK–WCN	,, ,,	,, ,, ,,
OK–WCO	,, ,,	,, ,, ,,
OK–WCP	,, ,,	,, ,, ,,
OK–WCR	,, ,,	,, ,, ,,
OK–WCS	,, ,,	,, ,, ,,
OK–WCT	Douglas C–47	,, ,, ,,
OK–WDA	,, ,,	,, ,, ,,
OK–WDC	,, ,,	,, ,, ,,
OK–WDD	,, ,,	,, ,, ,,
OK–WDE	,, ,,	,, ,, ,,
OK–WDF	,, ,,	,, ,, ,,
OK–WDG	,, ,,	,, ,, ,,
OK–WDH	,, ,,	,, ,, ,,
OK–WDI	,, ,,	,, ,, ,,
OK–WDJ	,, ,,	,, ,, ,,
OK–WDK	,, ,,	,, ,, ,,
OK–WDL	,, ,,	,, ,, ,,
OK–WDN	,, ,,	,, ,, ,,
OK–WDO	,, ,,	,, ,, ,,
OK–WDP	,, ,,	,, ,, ,,
OK–WDQ	,, ,,	,, ,, ,,
OK–WDR	,, ,,	,, ,, ,,
OK–WDS	,, ,,	,, ,, ,,
OK–WDT	,, ,,	,, ,, ,,
OK–WDU	,, ,,	,, ,, ,,
OK–WDV	,, ,,	,, ,, ,,
OK–WDW	,, ,,	,, ,, ,,
OK–WDY	,, ,,	,, ,, ,,
OK–WDZ	,, ,,	,, ,, ,,
OK–XDG	,, ,,	,, ,, ,,
OK–XDH	,, ,,	,, ,, ,,
OK–XDN	,, ,,	,, ,, ,,

BELGIUM (OO)

OO–APC	Douglas C–47	Cobeta
OO–APG	Avro 19	,,
OO–API	Hudson	,,

Registration	Type	Owner or Operator
OO-AUL	Douglas DC-3	Sabena
OO-AUM	,, ,,	,,
OO-AUN	,, ,,	,,
OO-AUO	,, ,,	,,
OO-AUP	,, ,,	,,
OO-AUV	,, ,,	,,
OO-AUW	Douglas C-47	,,
OO-AUX	,, DC-3	,,
OO-AUY	,, ,,	,,
OO-AUZ	,, ,,	,,
OO-AWA	,, DC-6	,,
OO-AWB	,, ,,	,,
OO-AWC	,, ,,	,,
OO-AWF	,, C-47	,,
OO-AWG	,, DC-3	,,
OO-AWJ	,, C-47	,,
OO-AWK	,, ,,	,,
OO-AWL	,, DC-3	,,
OO-AWM	,, C-47	,,
OO-AWO	Convair-Liner	,,
OO-AWP	,, ,,	,,
OO-AWQ	,, ,,	,,
OO-AWR	,, ,,	,,
OO-AWS	,, ,,	,,
OO-AWT	,, ,,	,,
OO-CBA	Douglas DC-3	,,
OO-CBB	,, ,,	,,
OO-CBC	,, ,,	,,
OO-CBN	Douglas C-47	,,
OO-SBC	,, DC-3	,,
OO-SBD	,, ,,	,,
OO-UBJ	,, ,,	,,
OO-UBT	,, C-47	,,

DENMARK (OY)

OY-AAE	Douglas DC-6	Scandinavian Airlines System			*Skjalm*
OY-AAF	,, ,,	,,	,,	,,	*Skjold*
OY-DFI	,, DC-4	,,	,,	,,	*Dan*
OY-DFO	,, ,,	,,	,,	,,	*Rolf*

N.B.—Scandinavian Airlines System aircraft names are all suffixed Viking

NETHERLANDS (PH)

PH-TAU	Constellation L49	K.L.M. *Utrecht*
PH-TAV	,,	,, *Venlo*
PH-TAY	Douglas C-47A	,,
PH-TAZ	,, ,,	,,
PH-TBH	,, ,,	,,
PH-TBI	,, ,,	,,

Registration	Type	Owner or Operator
PH–TBK	Douglas C–47A	K.L.M.
PH–TBL	,, ,,	,,
PH–TBM	,, ,,	,,
PH–TBP	,, ,,	,,
PH–TBY	,, ,,	,,
PH–TBZ	,, ,,	,,
PH–TCB	,, ,,	,,
PH–TCE	Douglas DC–4	,, Edam
PH–TCI	,, C–47A	,,
PH–TCK	,, ,,	,,
PH–TCL	,, ,,	,,
PH–TCS	,, ,,	,,
PH–TCT	,, ,,	,,
PH–TCU	,, ,,	,,
PH–TCY	,, ,,	,,
PH–TDA	Constellation L–49	,, Arnhem
PH–TDB	Constellation L749	,, Walcheren
PH–TDC	,, ,,	,, Curacao
PH–TDD	,, ,,	,, Delft
PH–TDE	,, ,,	,, Eindhoven
PH–TDG	,, ,,	,, Gouda
PH–TDH	,, ,,	,, Holland
PH–TDI	,, ,,	,, Enschede
PH–TDK	,, ,,	,, Amsterdam
PH–TDL	Douglas C–54B	,, Groningen
PH–TDM	,, ,,	,, Aalsmeer
PH–TDN	Constellation L–749A	,, Vlaardingen
PH–TDO	,, ,,	,, Maastricht
PH–TDU	Douglas C–47A	,,
PH–TDV	,, ,,	,,
PH–TDW	,, ,,	,,
PH–TDZ	,, ,,	,,
PH–TEA	Convair-Liner	,, Adriaan van Ostade
PH–TEB	,, ,,	,, Rembrandt
PH–TEC	,, ,,	,, Albert Cuyp
PH–TED	,, ,,	,, Gerard Terboch
PH–TEE	,, ,,	,, Jan Steen
PH–TEF	,, ,,	,, Frans Hals
PH–TEG	,, ,,	,, Jan van Goyen
PH–TEH	,, ,,	,, Pieter de Hooch
PH–TEI	,, ,,	,, Paulus Potter
PH–TEK	,, ,,	,, Johannes Vermeer
PH–TEL	,, ,,	,, Jacob van Ruisdael
PH–TEM	,, ,,	,, Meindert Hobbema
PH–TEP	Constellation L–749	,, Pontianak
PH–TES	,, ,,	,, Soerabaja
PH–TET	,, ,,	,, Tilburg
PH–TEY	Douglas C–54B	,, Limburg
PH–TEZ	,, ,,	,, Zeeland

PHILIPPINES (PI)

PI–C290	Douglas DC–6	Philippine Air Lines Bataan
PI–C291	,, ,,	,, ,, ,, Layte
PI–C292	,, ,,	,, ,, ,, Lingayen
PI–C293	,, ,,	,, ,, ,, Manila
PI–C294	,, ,,	,, ,, ,, Mindoro

BRAZIL (PP)

Registration	Type	Owner or Operator
PP–PCB	Constellation	Panair do Brasil
PP–PCF	,,	,, ,, ,,
PP–PCG	,,	,, ,, ,,
PP–PCR	,,	,, ,, ,,
PP–PDA	,.	,, ,, ,,

SWEDEN (SE)

SE–BBA	Douglas DC–4	Scandinavian Airlines System			Sigtrygg
SE–BBC	,, ,,	,,	,,	,,	Sigvard
SE–BBD	,, ,,	,,	,,	,,	Sigmund
SE–BBE	,, ,,	,,	,,	,,	Svavar
SE–BBF	,, ,,	,,	,,	,,	Sverker
SE–BDB	Douglas DC–6	,,	,,	,,	Agne
SE–BDC	,, ,,	,,	,,	,,	Alf
SE–BDD	,, ,,	,,	,,	,,	Algaut
SE–BDE	,, ,,	,,	,,	,,	Alrek
SE–BDF	,, ,,	,,	,,	,,	Alvar
SE–BDL	,, ,,	,,	,,	,,	Asmund
SE–BDM	,, ,,	,,	,,	,,	Anund
SE–BDO	,, ,,	,,	,,	,,	Arngrim

N.B.—Scandinavian Airlines System aircraft names are suffixed Viking

GREECE (SX)

SX–DAA	Liberator	Hellenic Airlines Maid of Athens
SX–DAB	,,	,, ,,

ICELAND (TF)

TF–ISE	Douglas C–54	Flugfelag Islands H.F. Gullfaxi
TF–RVC	,, ,,	Loftleidir H.F. Geysir
TF–RVH	,, ,,	,, ,, Hekla

AUSTRALIA (VH)

VH–EAA	Constellation	Qantas Empire Airways Ross Smith
VH–EAB	,,	,, ,, ,, Lawrence Hargrave

Registration	Type	Owner or Operator
VH–EAC	Constellation	Qantas Empire Airways *Harry Hawker*
VH–EAD	,,	,, ,, ,, *Charles Kingsford Smith*
VH–	,,	,, ,, ,,
VH–EBK	Douglas C–54	,, ,, ,,
VH–EBL	,, ,,	,, ,, ,,
VH–EBM	,, ,,	,, ,, ,,

CEYLON (VP)

VP–CBD	Douglas C–54	Air Ceylon *Laxapana*
VP–CBE	,, ,,	,, *Ratmalana*

INDIA (VT)

VT–CQP	Constellation	Air India International *Malabar*
VT–CQS	,,	,, ,, ,, *Moghul*
VT–DAR	,,	,, ,, ,, *Maratha*
VT–DAS	,,	,, ,, ,, *Himalayan*

N.B.—Air India International Constellations are suffixed Princess

IRAQ (YI)

YI–ABP	Viking IB	Iraqi Airways *Al Mahfoutah*
YI–ABQ	,, ,,	,, ,, *Al Maanounah*
YI–ABR	,, ,,	,, ,, *Al Mamica*

SOUTH AFRICA (ZS)

ZS–AUA	Douglas DC–4	South African Airways *Tafelberg*
ZS–AUB	,, ,,	,, ,, ,, *Outeniqua*
ZS–AUC	,, ,,	,, ,, ,, *Drakensberg*
ZS–BMF	,, ,,	,, ,, ,, *Amatola*
ZS–BMG	,, ,,	,, ,, ,, *Magaliesberg*
ZS–BMH	,, ,,	,, ,, ,, *Lebombo*
ZS–BWN	,, ,,	,, ,, ,, *Swartberg*
ZS–	Constellation	,, ,, ,,
ZS–	,,	,, ,, ,,
ZS–	,,	,, ,, ,,
ZS–	,,	,, ,, ,,

(Concluded on page 70

CIVIL AIRCRAFT SPECIFICATIONS

AIRCRAFT	MANUFACTURER	ENGINES	SEATS	SPAN	Loaded Wt. (lb.)	Cruising Speed M.P.H.
Aeronca 100	Aeronca (G.B.)	1×36 J.A.P.	2	36'	1,005	70
Aerovan	Miles (G.B.)	2×155 Cirrus Major	9/Freight	50'	5,800	110
Air Horse Hel.	Cierva (G.B.)	1×1,620 Merlin	24	95'	17,500	95
Ambassador	Airspeed (G.B.)	2×2,700 Centaurus	49	115'	52,000	245
Anson I	A.V. Roe (G.B.)	2×320 Cheetah	9	56' 6"	7,663	158
Apollo	Armst. Whit. (G.B.)	4×1,000+320 lb. Mamba	24-41	92'	43,000	276
Argus	Fairchild (U.S.A.)	1×165 Super Scarab	4	36' 4"	2,801	104
Arrow	Auster (G.B.)	1×75 Continental	2	36'	1,450	87
Auster 5	" "	1×130 Lycoming	2-3	36'	1,920	112
Auster J/4	" "	1×90 Cirrus	2	36'	1,600	92
Autocar	" "	1×130 Gipsy Major	4	36'	1,850	106
Autocrat	" "	1×100 Cirrus Minor	3	36'		100
Avro XIX	A.V. Roe (G.B.)	1×420 Cheetah	6-9	56' 6"		155
Beaver	De Havilland (Canada)	1×450 Wasp Junior	4-7	48'	4,500	146
Brabazon I	Bristol (G.B.)	8×2,650 Centaurus	101	230'	290,000	250
Bristol Type 170	" "	2×1,780 Hercules	36/Freight	108'	40,000	162
Bristol Type 171 Hel.	" "	1×550 Leonides	4	48' 7" Dia.	5,200	
C.30 A Autogiro	Cierva (G.B.)	1×140 Genet Major	2	37'	1,900	85
Canadair Four	Canadair (Canada)	4×1,760 Merlin	40	117' 6"	82,300	302
Chipmunk	De Havilland (G.B.)	1×140 Gipsy Major	2	34' 4"	1,900	113
Comet	" "	4×5,000 lb. Ghost	36-48	115'	105,000	490
Constellation 749A	Lockheed (U.S.A.)	4×2,500 Cyclone	44-64	123'	107,000	309
Consul	Airspeed (G.B.)	2×395 Cheetah	5-6	53' 4"	8,250	156
Convair-Liner	Consolidated (U.S.A.)	2×2,400 P & W R-2800	40	91' 9"	40,500	291
Cub	Piper (U.S.A.)	1×65 Continental	2	35' 2"	1,220	75
DC-3 Dakota	Douglas (U.S.A.)	2×1,200 P & W R-1830	21-32	95'	25,200	207
DC-4 Skymaster	" "	4×1,350 P & W R-2000	36-47	117' 6"	73,000	231
DC-6	" "	4×2,150 P & W R-2800	52-68	117' 6"	93,200	285
Dove	De Havilland (G.B.)	2×345 Gipsy Queen	8-11	57'	8,500	179
Gemini	Miles (G.B.)	2×100 Cirrus Minor	4	36' 2"	3,000	135
Halifax	Handley Page (G.B.)	4×1,650 Hercules	11/Freight	104'	65,000	270
Hawk Major	Miles (G.B.)	1×130 Gipsy Major	2	33'	1,800	135
Hawk Trainer 3	" "	1×130 Gipsy Major	2	33' 10"	1,900	120
Hermes 4	Handley Page (G.B.)	4×2,100 Hercules	40-74	113'	82,000	252

Aircraft	Makers	Engines	Accom.	Span	Weight (lb.)	Speed (m.p.h.)
Hermes 5	Handley Page (G.B.)	4 × 2,430 Theseus	40-74	113'	86,000	343
Hornet Moth	De Havilland (G.B.)	1 × 130 Gipsy Moth	2	31' 11"	2,000	105
IL-12	Ilyushin (Russia)	2 × 1,800 Ash-82	27-32	104'	38,000	217
Lancastrian	A.V. Roe (G.B.)	4 × 1,280 Merlin	9/Freight	102'	45,364	285
Languedoc	S.N.C.A.S.E. (France)	4 × 1,220 Gnome-Rhone	12-33	96' 5"	65,000	233
Liberator	Consolidated (U.S.A.)	4 × 1,200 P & W R-1830	16-20/F.	110'	56,000	215
Lodestar	Lockheed (U.S.A.)	2 × 1,200 Cyclone	14	65' 8"	18,500	200
M-18	Miles (G.B.)	1 × 150 Gipsy Major	2	31'	1,918	120
Marathon 1	Handley Page (G.B.)	4 × 150 Gipsy Queen	14-20	65'	18,000	209
Marathon 2	" "	2 × 1,270+384 lb. Mamba	14-20	65'		256
Messenger	Miles (G.B.)	1 × 155 Cirrus Major	3-4	36' 2"	2,400	112
Moth Minor	De Havilland (G.B.)	1 × 90 Gipsy Minor	2	36' 7"	1,550	100
Primer	Fairey (G.B.)	1 × 135 Gipsy Major	2	32' 10"	1,960	122
Prince	Percival (G.B.)	2 × 520 Leonides	8-10	56'	10,650	179
Proctor 5	"	1 × 208 Gipsy Queen	4	39' 6"	3,500	140
Pup	Sopwith (G.B.)	1 × 80 Le Rhone	—	26' 6"	1,225	100
Q-6	Percival (G.B.)	2 × 205 Gipsy Six	6	46' 8"	5,550	181
Rapide	De Havilland (G.B.)	2 × 200 Gipsy Six	5-8	48'	5,550	132
Sandringham 5	Short (G.B.)	4 × 1,200 P & W R-1830	22	112' 9"	56,000	204
Sealand	"	2 × 350 Gipsy Queen	5-8	59'	9,100	181
Sea Otter	Vickers (G.B.)	1 × 805 Mercury	5	46'	10,000	100
Sikorsky S-51 Hel.	Westland (G.B.)	1 × 505 Leonides	4	48' Dia.	5,374	85
Skeeter Hel.	Cierva (G.B.)	1 × 145 Gipsy Major	2	32' Dia.	1,800	73
Sky Jeep	Chrislea (G.B.)	1 × 155 Cirrus Major	2	36'	2,400	110
SM. 95	SIAI-Marchetti (Italy)	4 × 1,215 Twin Wasp	30-38	112' 5"	47,600	215
Solent	Short (G.B.)	4 × 1,795 Hercules	24-39	112' 9"	78,000	236
Spitfire Trainer	Vickers (G.B.)	1 × 1,325 Merlin	2	36' 10"	7,400	232
Stratocruiser	Boeing (U.S.A.)	4 × 3,500 P & W R-4360	55-80	141' 3"	142,000	340
Sunderland 3	Short (G.B.)	4 × 1,065 Pegasus	22	112' 9"	55,000	115
Super Ace 2	Chrislea (G.B.)	1 × 145 Gipsy Major	4	36'	2,350	112
Swallow	British Aircraft (G.B.)	1 × 80 Pobjoy 8	1	42' 8"	1,500	92
Swift	Comper (G.B.)	1 × 90 Cirrus Minor	2	24'	985	110
Taylorcraft D	Taylorcraft (G.B.)	1 × 130 Gipsy Major	1	36'	1,400	107
Tiger Moth	De Havilland (G.B.)	1 × 130 Gipsy Major	2	29' 4"	1,825	94
Tipsy Trainer	Tipsy (G.B.)	1 × 52 Mikron	1	31' 2"	1,200	100
Tudor 5	A.V. Roe (G.B.)	4 × 1,740 Merlin	44	120'	80,000	285
Vega Gull	Percival (G.B.)	1 × 200 Gipsy Six	4	39' 6"	3,250	170
Viking	Vickers (G.B.)	2 × 1,690 Hercules	27	89' 3"	34,000	210
Viscount 700	Vickers (G.B.)	4 × 1,420+325 lb. Dart	40-53	94'	48,000	326
Whitney Straight	Miles (G.B.)	1 × 130 Gipsy Major	2	35' 8"	1,896	130
York	A.V. Roe (G.B.)	4 × 1,280 Merlin	12-56	102'	68,597	255

Registration	Type	Owner or Operator
4X–ACC	Douglas DC–4	El Al Rechovoth
4X–ACD	,, ,,	,, ,, Herzel

MILITARY REGISTRATIONS

MILITARY aircraft, like their civil counterparts, all carry some kind of identification markings, and these " serial numbers," as they are usually called, form the basis of a fascinating but complicated study. Although they are really outside the scope of this book, the following notes are included to help readers to understand how military serial numbers are allocated and how they can be distinguished from civil registrations.

Serial numbers for aircraft operated by the Royal Air Force and the Air Branch of the Royal Navy are allocated by a department of the Ministry of Supply in a co-ordinated system. Each serial consists of a five-symbol group, made up of either one letter followed by four digits or, more recently, two letters followed by three digits. Through the years, they have run progressively, starting with the prefix A, then B, C, etc., through to Z, which was followed by the AA prefix, then AB, etc., up to WF, which is in use as this book goes to press.

The serial number on R.A.F. and R.N. aircraft is displayed on each side of the rear fuselage and beneath each wing, in addition to the national red, white and blue roundels. Such a serial number is, therefore, readily distinguishable and can be ignored by those using this book as a means of identifying civil aircraft types.

The Ministry of Supply, in its capacity of foster-mother to many of the civil prototypes developed in this country since the war, has allocated military-type serials to most of these prototypes for the period of their testing by its test pilots. These same aircraft also receive normal civil registrations, however, and these are included in the appropriate section of this book.

Military aircraft of other countries also can be seen flying over the United Kingdom. The identification systems of these various countries are too diverse to be dealt with here, but, as a rule, military aircraft can be quickly identified by national insignia on their wings and fuselage. Furthermore, an identification marking which does not fit into the scheme of national civil markings as laid down in this book can be assumed to be a military serial.

Left: Comper SWIFT. Although the oldest 'plane in the 1949 King's Cup race and flown by the youngest pilot, G–ABUS gained third place. *(F.G. Swanborough.)*

Right: B.A. SWALLOW. Based on the old German Klemm design, the Swallow was one of the lowest priced pre-war two-seaters. *(F. G. Swanborough.)*

Left: de Havilland HORNET MOTH Last of the famous de Havilland Moth biplanes, the Hornet Moth is a cabin two-seater. *(F. G. Swanborough.)*

Right: Miles M–18. A development of the better-known Magister (Hawk Trainer 3), only a few M–18's were built.

Above : Cierva AIR HORSE
World's largest helicopter,
the Air Horse was designed
to carry 24 passengers or
3 tons of freight. (*John W. R.
Taylor.*)

Left : Cierva C.30A. Auto
giros of this type were used
during the war for radar
calibration work. (*John W. R.
Taylor.*)

Below : Sikorsky S–51.
G–ALEI has been specially
fitted out with crop-spraying
equipment by Pest Control
Ltd. Other S–51's are used
by B.E.A. for passenger and
mail carrying.